101 QUESTIONS

ABOUT FOOD AND DIGESTION THAT HAVE BEEN EATING AT YOU ... UNTIL NOW

101 QUESTIONS ABOUT FOOD AND DIGESTION

THAT HAVE BEEN EATING AT YOU ...UNTIL NOW

· · · ·

FAITH HICKMAN BRYNIE

· · · ·

Twenty-First Century Books

BROOKFIELD, CONNECTICUT

Published by Twenty-First Century Books
A Division of The Millbrook Press, Inc.
2 Old New Milford Road
Brookfield, Connecticut 06804

Cover photograph courtesy of © Michael Carroll/The Stock Illustration Source

Photographs courtesy of Photo Researchers, Inc.: pp. 23 (© Dr. E. Walker/SPL), 28 (© Prof. P. Motta/
Department of Anatomy/University La Sapienza, Rome/SPL), 56 (© Prof. P. Motta/Department of
Anatomy/University La Sapienza, Rome/SPL), 67 (right © Biophoto Associates), 68 (top left © Oliver
Meckes; top right © Edward Gray/SPL; bottom right © Sinclair Stammers/SPL), 72 (© SPL);
Ormond MacDougald/University of Michigan: p. 62 (both); Visuals Unlimited: pp. 67 (left © S.I.U.), 97
(© D. Yeske), 110 (© Science VU), 141 (© S.I.U.); Bruce Coleman, Inc.: p. 68 (bottom left © Bob
Gossington); Friends of Celiac Disease Association: p. 73 (© Mike Tobin); AP/Wide World Photos: p. 86;
© Martin Schwalbe: p. 116; © 2001 Fred C. Fussell: p. 119; © Randy Glasbergen **www.glasbergen.com**:
p. 140

Library of Congress Cataloging-in-Publication Data
Brynie, Faith Hickman, 1946-
101 questions about food and digestion that have been eating at you—until now / Faith Hickman Brynie
p. cm.
Includes bibliographical references and index.
Summary: Questions and answers explain the human digestive system and how it uses food for nutrition.
ISBN 0-7613-2309-0 (lib. bdg.)
1. Nutrition—Juvenile literature. 2. Digestion—Juvenile literature. [1. Digestion—Miscellanea.
2. Digestive system—Miscellanea. 3. Nutrition—Miscellanea. 4. Questions and answers.] I. Title: One
hundred one questions about food and digestion that have been eating at you—until now.
QP141 .B884 2002
612.3'9—dc21 2001052250

Data for the Vegetable Eating and Stroke Risk chart on page 43 and the Vitamin C and Stroke Risk
chart on page 44 from Tetsuji Yokoyama, Chigusa Date, Yoshihiro Kokubo, Nobuo Yoshiike, Yasuhiro
Matsumura, and Heizo Tanaka. "Serum Vitamin C Concentration Was Inversely Associated With
Subsequent 20-Year Incidence of Stroke in a Japanese Rural Community: The Shibata Study," *Stroke*,
2000: 31-2287-2294.

Data for the map on page 75 from M. Karronen, M. Viik-Kajander, E. Moltchanova, I. Libman, R.
LaPorte, and J. Tuomilehto, "Incidence of Childhood Type 1 Diabetes Worldwide," *Diabetes Care*
(2000), p. 1516-26.

CONTENTS

The author is grateful to the following teachers and their students for the questions they contributed to this volume: Mark Stephansky, Whitman-Hanson Regional High School, Whitman, Massachusetts; Jill Losee-Hoehlein, Great Bridge High School, Chesapeake, Virginia; and Kim Cheek, Medway Middle School, Medway, Massachusetts.

The author greatly appreciates the thorough and thoughtful critical reviews prepared by Dr. Jack Davis, internist in private practice, Kalispell, Montana; Jennifer Janetski, MS, RD, Outpatient Dietitian, Kalispell Regional Medical Center; and Dr. Joseph Fiorito, a gastroenterologist at Danbury Hospital, Danbury, Connecticut.

Special thanks also to Amy Shields for expanding the series and believing in its author. And, as always, my gratitude to Lloyd for being Lloyd and Ann for being Ann.

FOREWORD

It's a very odd thing—
As odd as can be—
That whatever Miss T eats
Turns into Miss T.

• WALTER DE LA MARE •

My friend the mathematician beamed with pride at the mention of his newborn daughter. Taking a lead from Walter de la Mare, he called her Miss T.

In the early weeks of Miss T's life, my friend estimated that—if her growth continued at its present rate—she'd stand 17 feet (518 centimeters) tall and weigh more than two tons by the time she was three. Joking that he would have to tether her in the backyard like a circus elephant, he exclaimed: "Can you believe it? She's made of nothing but milk!"

We laughed at her father's silliness as we oohed and aahed over the baby, but we had to admit he had a point. The infant was indeed growing rapidly, and the only source of energy and raw materials was her mother's milk.

As time went on, her father's prediction of her toddler size proved wrong, but Miss T did continue to grow. She was built first from milk . . . and then cereal . . . and then bananas . . . and, before long, potatoes.

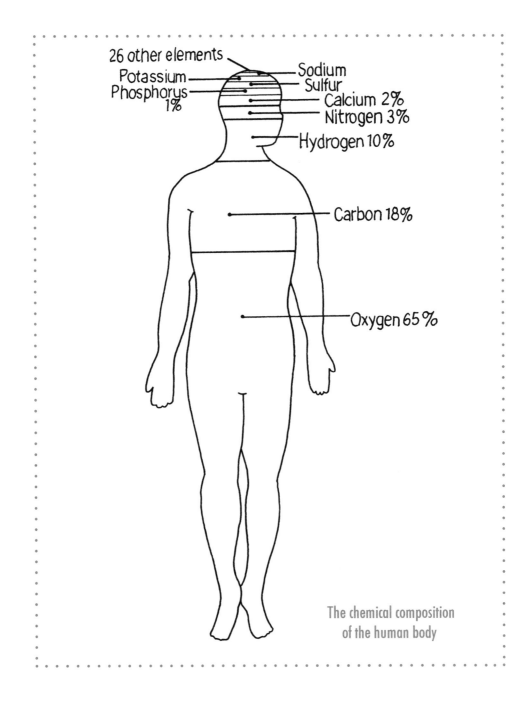

26 other elements
Potassium
Phosphorus
1%
Sodium
Sulfur
Calcium 2%
Nitrogen 3%
Hydrogen 10%

Carbon 18%

Oxygen 65%

The chemical composition
of the human body

Especially potatoes. She loved them. In that, too, my friend found a literary connection: "Pray for peace and grace and spiritual food," wrote J. T. Pettee, a nineteenth-century American writer, "for wisdom and guidance, for all these are good—but don't forget the potatoes."

Miss T and her potatoes are made from the same elements found in earth, air, and water. She's mostly oxygen, carbon, hydrogen, and nitrogen. The "bricks and mortar" of Miss T's body are the proteins. Proteins are chains of smaller units called amino acids. Miss T's body rearranges the amino acids in her food to form the two kinds of proteins that are Miss T. The first are her structural proteins: bones, blood, muscle, and brain. The second are her enzymes. Enzymes accelerate chemical reactions, including the manufacture of other proteins. More than 3,000 different enzymes keep Miss T's body chemistry going.[1]

Today, having grown with grace and wisdom and potatoes, Miss T is a high-school student. She prefers low-fat yogurt to milk, and but she knows her father was right. She is made from the foods she eats. Food builds her muscle, bone, and blood. It powers her every activity, from studying for tests to running on the track team.

Her dad still calls her Miss T, but now it means "Miss Terrific."

Miss T laughs when he calls her that. "It's just simple chemistry," she says.

CHAPTER ONE

21 QUESTIONS

THAT SHOULD
COME FIRST

*EAT: To perform successively (and successfully) the functions of
mastication, humectation, and deglutition.*

• AMBROSE BIERCE, *THE DEVIL'S DICTIONARY* •

What Is Food,
and How Does
the Body Use
It?

Column A: Food	Column B: Function
carbohydrate	growth
fat	repair
protein	energy

The body uses (*column A*) for (*column B*). Fill in the blanks with any
two choices. You'll be right every time!

Foods are either carbohydrates (sugars and starches), fats (and oils),
or proteins (tissue-building materials that contain nitrogen). Each provides the energy and raw materials that sustain life, growth, and repair.

Water, vitamins, and minerals are important nutrients, but they are not classified as foods because they do not provide energy.

The body is like a factory. In a factory, builders and maintenance personnel use boards, bricks, and shingles to build and repair the structure. The same thing happens in the body. It uses the materials from food to grow, repair damage, and rectify wear and tear. In a factory, workers bring in a fuel such as coal or gas to power their machines and make their goods. For a body, the fuel is food. It, too, must be brought in. Carbohydrates and fats (and sometimes proteins) provide the energy that powers the body's activities.

A lot goes on inside a factory that isn't apparent in the manufactured product. In manufacturing, for example, petroleum must be broken down into smaller molecules to make plastic. Metals must be extracted from ore to make steel. In a similar fashion, food molecules in the body must be broken into their basic building blocks. Then new molecules are fashioned from the raw materials that food provides.

The business of a factory is constructing, packaging, storing, and distributing a product. The business of a living body is making and repairing cell parts, moving materials from place to place, heating and moving the body, getting rid of wastes, and more. The body is more self-contained and self-sufficient than any factory. Before making its products, it actually builds its own tools. The tools are enzymes, the proteins that speed up chemical reactions in living cells.

What's the Difference Between Digestion and Metabolism?

Digestion is the breakdown of large food molecules into smaller ones. It happens in the digestive organs, mostly in the small intestine. There, enzymes cut large carbohydrate molecules into their basic building block, the simple sugar called glucose. They dismantle fats into their two basic parts, fatty acids and glycerol. They split proteins into amino acids, any of 20 different kinds.

Metabolism includes all the chemical reactions needed to fuel and maintain the body. It is the release and use of energy from food molecules. You cannot see food energy, but you can see and feel its effects in the movement and warmth of the body.

The release of energy from food occurs in every cell. Specialized organelles called mitochondria are the cell's "power plants." There, enzymes break down glucose, and sometimes other food materials, into (eventually) carbon dioxide and water. A series of chemical reactions creates molecules of the body's main energy compound, ATP (for adenosine triphosphate).

A lot of energy is stored in the bonds that hold the three phosphate groups onto this molecule. (A phosphate group is a unit made of one phosphorus atom and four oxygen atoms.) When enzymes break those bonds, that energy is released and the cell can use it. The cell is an efficient recycler. It breaks the bonds one at a time until it gets to AMP, or adenosine monophosphate—an adenosine with only one phosphate group attached. It then reuses the AMP, building it back up again for reuse as ATP.

How Do Enzymes Break Down Food Molecules?

All digestive enzymes break chemical bonds the same way. They insert a water molecule into a bond between atoms. The name for this process is hydrolysis (meaning, literally, "water split"). Table sugar, for example, is sucrose. It is made of two simple sugar molecules, glucose and fructose, hooked together. The enzyme sucrase locks onto the sucrose

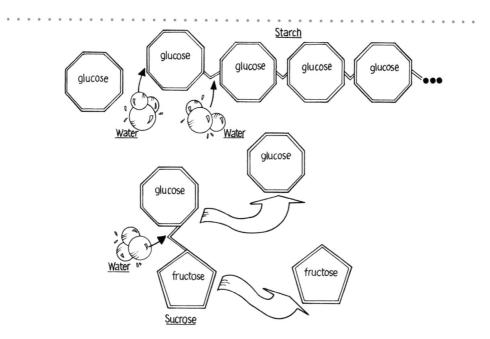

Water breaks a large starch molecule into its building block of the simple sugar glucose. The process is called hydrolysis. Hydrolysis splits table sugar (sucrose) into the simple sugars glucose and fructose.

molecule. Then it inserts a molecule of water into the bond between the two simple sugar units. The water splits and separates them, releasing energy in the process.

What Foods Are Carbohydrates, and How Does the Body Use them?

Carbohydrates are made from only three elements: carbon, hydrogen, and oxygen. Different arrangements of atoms of these elements form different compounds, ranging from the starch in potatoes and rice to the sugars in milk and fruits. Plants store the sun's energy in the bonds of the glucose molecule, which they make from carbon dioxide and water. They then hook glucose units together in larger molecules of starch. Plants store starch in seeds, fruits, and cereal grains—as well as in the specialized storage cells of root vegetables such as carrots and beets.

Carbohydrates are the basic foods from which all others are made. Both plants and animals rearrange the molecules of simple sugars into fats and proteins. Most carbohydrates digest easily. An exception is cellulose, a long chain of more than 3,000 glucose molecules. It forms the cell walls of most plants. It doesn't dissolve in water. Humans lack the enzyme needed to break it down.

What Foods Are Fats, and How Does the Body Use Them?

Like carbohydrates, fats are made of carbon, hydrogen, and oxygen. Fats in foods are either solid at room temperature (animal lard, vegetable shortening, the hidden fats in meats, eggs, cheese, and fish) or liquid (vegetable and fish oils, the fat in whole milk, oil in olives). Chemically, fats and oils are made mostly of molecules called triglycerides. These units are themselves composed of smaller units: three molecules of fatty acids attached to one molecule of glycerol.

The body stores most of its fat reserves as triglycerides. Having broken them apart in the small intestine, the body puts them back together again in the liver. From the liver, fat reserves can be sent to all body cells where they are used for growth and maintenance, as well as for an energy source. Fatty acids provide about 40 percent of the body's total energy requirement. For the heart muscle, they may provide as much as 60 to 80 percent.[1]

The word protein comes from the Greek *proteios*, meaning "holding first place." Proteins are found in foods from animals such as meat, milk, and eggs. They are also abundant in some plant foods such as beans, peas, and nuts.

Although the human body needs only a little protein compared with carbohydrates and fats, amino acids are essential in building and maintaining the body. Plants can make all of the amino acids for themselves. Humans and other animals cannot. Of more than 100 amino acids that occur in nature, only 20 types are common in proteins. Humans can make 11 of them, but they must get 9 from their food.[2]

In proteins, amino acids are strung in chains, like beads. Protein molecules are one or more of these long chains. The chains twist into the three-dimensional shape of a complete protein. The amino acids they contain and the shapes they form give proteins different properties, meaning that the proteins in muscle and blood differ from those in skin and bone, both in how they are built and in what they do.

Body cells use amino acids to build connective tissue such as the tendons that hold muscle to bone, as well as bone and muscle themselves. Hemoglobin, the molecule in blood that carries oxygen from the lungs to all body cells, is a protein. Yet another protein is keratin. It makes hair strong and nails tough.

The largest amount of protein in the human body is in muscle. About half of normal body weight is muscle, and about half the body's total protein is incorporated in muscle. That means a 150-pound (70-kilogram) adult contains about 38 pounds (17 kilograms) of muscle protein.[3]

Some hormones are proteins. Hormones are molecules made by one organ that affect another. Some hormones directly influence the building and repair of the body. For example, the pituitary gland in the brain produces both the thyroid-stimulating hormone (TSH, or thyrotropin) and a growth hormone. TSH causes the thyroid gland to release yet another hormone that regulates the rate of energy use in cells. Growth hormone causes cells to make RNA from DNA. That is the first step in making the proteins from which new and bigger cells are made.

What Does Saliva Do? Saliva contains the enzyme amylase. This enzyme helps break starch into sugar, but it's not an important part of digestion. More significant is the role of saliva in lubricating food and making it easier to swallow.

The main benefit of saliva is protecting the mouth and the body against invading microorganisms. Nearly 500 species of microbes, most of them harmless, live in the mouth. Saliva leaves the harmless inhabitants alone, while washing away viruses, bacteria, and yeast that can cause infections. Saliva causes the microbes to clump together so they are swallowed, to be killed by stomach acid. White blood cells that gobble up microbes are destroyed in the mouth, where they burst because their salt content is higher than that found in saliva. Saliva also contains enzymes that kill or inhibit the growth of disease-causing microbes.

Saliva protects the tissues of the mouth from erosion by acidic foods. It neutralizes acids that can eat holes in teeth, and flushes away the sugars and food particles that decay bacteria feed on. Minerals in saliva such as calcium and fluoride reverse the decay process, making teeth hard and strong.

Have you ever noticed that a cut in your mouth heals quickly? That's because saliva contains the compound EGF (for epidermal growth factor). It speeds repair and regrowth of tissues.

Leonardo da Vinci wrote: "Man and animals are merely a passage and channel for food." He was right. Compared with some other systems of the body, the digestive system is relatively simple. It's a tube. Food enters at one end. Waste materials exit at the other. Different parts of the tube have different forms and functions, and other organs outside the tube play a role.

The tube begins with the mouth, where the tongue tastes food and mixes it, while the teeth break it into smaller pieces. Although chewing isn't essential for digestion, it makes digestive enzymes work better. How? Many small pieces of food expose more surface area to the environment than one large piece of the same amount. With a greater surface area exposed, digestive enzymes find more places to hook on.

Swallowing begins with the action of voluntary muscles, but it proceeds automatically after that. The epiglottis, a muscular flap at the back of the mouth, closes. It prevents food from going down the trachea (windpipe). The roof of the mouth rises to keep food from entering the nasal passages. Food passes down the throat into the esophagus. The rhythmic contractions of its muscular walls push food toward the stomach.

The stomach is muscular, too. It contracts strongly about three times a minute.[4] This churning mixes food with stomach acid and enzymes secreted from the stomach walls. Cells in the stomach wall secrete the enzyme pepsinogen. In the acid environment of the stomach, pepsinogen changes to pepsin. Pepsin breaks proteins into shorter chains of amino acids. Pepsin is responsible for about 10 to 20 percent of protein digestion.[5] It is the only enzyme that breaks down collagen, a protein found in the muscle, tendon, and skin of meats.

The amino-acid chains cleaved by pepsin stimulate stomach cells to release the hormone gastrin into the blood. Gastrin moves throughout

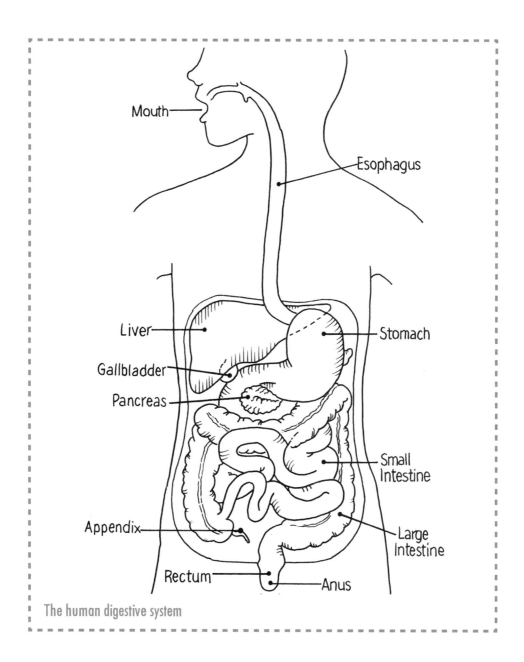

Mouth

Esophagus

Liver

Stomach

Gallbladder

Pancreas

Small Intestine

Appendix

Large Intestine

Rectum

Anus

The human digestive system

the body, returning to the stomach itself. There it triggers an increase in acid production and muscular contraction. It also stimulates the pancreas to make the enzymes needed for further digestion.

From the stomach, partially digested food passes into the first part of the small intestine, the duodenum. This is where most digestion occurs. The cells of the duodenal walls make some of the enzymes that work there. Other enzymes come through a duct from the pancreas. The pancreas is shaped like a "banana that has been stepped on. It has a slight curve to it, and it's about the same length, width, and thickness."[6] The pancreas secretes sodium bicarbonate (same compound as baking soda), which neutralizes some of the acid from the stomach.

Each enzyme at work in the small intestine speeds up a single kind of chemical change. For example, the enzyme maltase breaks apart the sugar maltose. Another enzyme, lactase, cleaves the sugar lactose. Trypsin is one of several enzymes that digest proteins. Each enzyme cuts the protein in a particular place until only single amino acids remain.

Several enzymes called lipases break apart fats. Lipases work only in the presence of bile acids. The liver produces bile. Bile is stored in the gallbladder until needed. It enters the duodenum through a duct from the gallbladder. Bile breaks up fat globules, creating many surfaces that can be attacked by lipase. Bile also helps eliminate excess cholesterol and dead red cells from the blood.

From the small intestine, undigested and indigestible materials pass into the colon, or large intestine. Little digestion occurs in the colon, but water is absorbed into the blood from the large intestine. There, also, bacteria continue the breakdown of some compounds and manufacture substances that the body can use. One example is vitamin K, a substance essential to blood clotting.

The semisolid wastes that remain are called feces. Fecal material collects in the colon and leaves the body through the anus. The indigestible cell walls of plants and damaged or worn-out cells from the walls of the digestive tract form a part of feces. Between one-third and one-half of fecal material is bacteria.[7]

What Causes Diarrhea?

As food moves through the digestive tract, the colon squeezes and relaxes, moving feces toward the anus. If the colon contracts too hard and too fast, food moves too rapidly for water to be absorbed into the blood. Diarrhea results, sometimes because of diet, but more often because of an infection by viruses or bacteria. The microbes multiply in the intestine and cause inflammation. The inflammation interferes with the absorption of nutrients through the wall of the small intestine. Water and minerals, such as sodium and potassium, leave the cells of the intestinal wall and combine with fecal material, causing loose stools or watery diarrhea.

What Causes Constipation?

Constipation is the opposite of diarrhea (see previous question). The colon pushes food too slowly. Too much water leaves the intestine, and the feces become hard and difficult to eliminate. Infections, stress, allergies, drugs, and poisons can slow the rate of colon contraction. So can eating too little fiber (found in fruits, vegetables, and whole grains) or drinking too little water.

Why Doesn't the Stomach Digest Itself?

The stomach would digest its own proteins were it not for the protective lining of mucus that its cells secrete. When too little mucus is produced or its

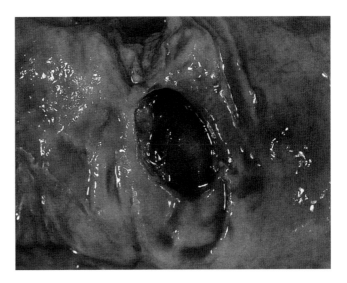

This bleeding gastric ulcer formed when stomach acid began to digest the lining of the stomach.

protective action fails, ulcers may form. Ulcers are sores in the stomach or intestines that do not heal. The acid and enzymes of the stomach eat into the stomach wall. In severe cases, they may eat completely through, causing a dangerous perforated ulcer. A bacterium, *Helicobacter pylori*, seems to play a role in this self-destructive process in many, if not most, ulcers. Certain drugs can cause ulcers, too.

How Do Food Molecules Get Out of the Digestive System?

In the small intestine, the building blocks of most foods pass through the intestinal wall into the bloodstream. (Only a few substances, such as alcohol and aspirin, are absorbed in the stomach.)

Villi are tiny, fingerlike projections of the intestinal wall. On them lie many, much smaller projections, the microvilli. The villi and microvilli increase the surface area of the lining by 600 times what it would be if the intestine were merely a

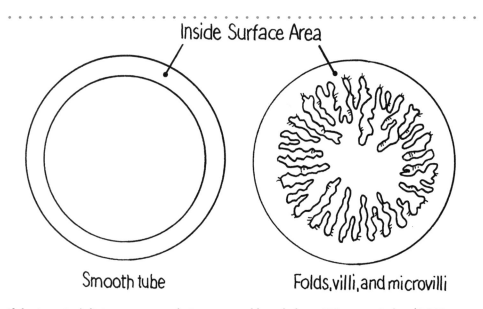

Inside Surface Area

Smooth tube   Folds, villi, and microvilli

If the intestine's lining were smooth, its area would total about 512 square inches (3,300 sq cm). The folds of the villi and microvilli increase the surface area some 600 times, for a total of about 310,000 square inches (2,000,000 sq cm).

smooth tube.[8] Countless capillaries (tiny blood vessels) lie inside the microvilli. Molecules can move through the outer surface of the microvilli, through the walls of the capillaries, and into the blood.

Some molecules can move into the blood by diffusion. Diffusion is the natural tendency of molecules to move from where there are many of them to where they are fewer in number. (Diffusion is the reason that air fresheners work. The scent molecules move out of the freshener and eventually spread evenly through the room.)

Diffusion isn't enough to move some larger molecules. It cannot move glucose either, because—at times—the concentration of glucose is greater in the blood than in the intestine. In these instances, a process called active transport does the job. Cells expend energy and use carrier enzymes to haul molecules through membranes.

Fat absorption requires still another mechanism. Enzymes in the intestine split away fatty acids from triglycerides. When two of the three fatty-acid chains are split off, a single fatty-acid chain attached to glycerol remains. This unit is called a monoglyceride.

The monoglyceride molecule lets the body handle fats—which cannot dissolve in water—as if they could. It has a soluble end (its "water-loving," or hydrophilic, tail) and a nonsoluble end (its "water-fearing," or hydrophobic, tail). In the intestine, bile salts arrange monoglyceride molecules into spheres, with their hydrophobic ends pointing in and their hydrophilic ends pointing out. Fatty acids and cholesterol find a home in the "dry" center of this structure, the micelle. The fat-soluble vitamins A, D, E, and K gather there, too.

The exterior, exposed surface of the micelle behaves like a water-soluble molecule. Carried along by water molecules that attach to its surface, the micelle passes into the cells that line the intestine. There the micelle breaks down and releases monoglycerides into the bloodstream. They travel to the liver where they are reassembled into triglycerides. The liver also collects and stores the fat-soluble vitamins that hitched a ride in the micelle. It removes them from the bloodstream when the supply is ample. It releases them later, when supplies run low.

How Is Energy in Foods Measured?

Most of the world measures food energy in kilojoules, a metric unit of force. In the United States, a unit of heat energy called the kilocalorie or (more simply) the calorie is commonly used. It is the amount of energy required to raise the temperature of one

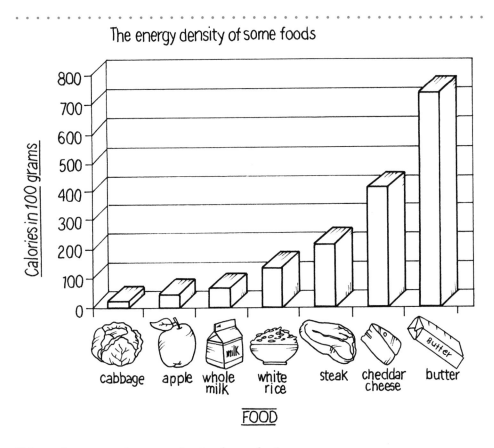

The energy density of some foods

Calories in 100 grams

| 800 |
| 700 |
| 600 |
| 500 |
| 400 |
| 300 |
| 200 |
| 100 |
| 0 |

cabbage   apple   whole milk   white rice   steak   cheddar cheese   butter

FOOD

This graph compares the energy density of some foods.

liter of water one degree Celsius (specifically from 15° to 16° C, or 59° to 61° Fahrenheit). A (kilo)calorie equals approximately 4.3 kilojoules.

By burning foods in sealed chambers called calorimeters, scientists can measure the amount of energy released when foods break down. The higher the caloric value of a food, the more energy it contains. Carbohydrate and protein foods supply about 4 kilocalories per gram (approximately 120 per ounce). Fats yield about 9 kilocalories per gram (about 270 per ounce).

Foods can be rated by their energy density. The greater the energy content (in kilojoules or calories) per unit of weight, the higher the energy density of the food. Thus, potato chips and candy bars are energy-dense foods. They contain a lot of energy in a small mass. Pasta, baked potatoes, and rice are lower in their energy density. Lowest of all are those foods that contain a lot of water, such as most fruits and vegetables. Energy density explains why six heads of lettuce supply the same energy as one chocolate bar.[9] Most of us would do well to eat fewer energy-dense foods.

What Makes Food Taste Good or Bad? Some 10,000 taste buds dot the tongue's rough surface.[10] Smaller numbers line the palate and throat. About a dozen taste cells operate inside each taste bud. Tiny hairs protrude from nerve cells through an opening in the bud called the taste pore. Saliva bathes each hair. When food enters the mouth, some of its molecules dissolve in saliva. When the molecules stimulate the taste hairs, the nerve cells generate chemicals called second messengers. (The food molecules themselves are the first messengers.) Second messengers change the taste cell's charge. A nerve impulse begins, sending a message to the brain. Taste buds react to six kinds of stimuli—sweet, sour, bitter, salty, fatty, and umami (MSG).

Without much success, scientists have tried to associate the shape, size, structure, electrical charge, or atomic weight of molecules with their taste. For example, investigators have found that bitter substances increase the amount of a second messenger called IP3, but how IP3 produces the perception of bitterness remains unknown.

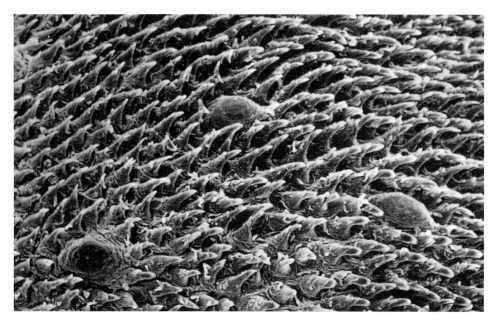

Each of the three round papillae shown here on the tongue's surface contains hundreds of taste buds. The smaller spiky structures help move food. (Magnified 70x)

Another second messenger is called cyclic AMP. Taste-testing laboratory mice cannot taste without it, but how it works is a mystery.

Much of what we perceive as flavor is actually smell. Chewing releases molecules that travel up the back of the throat into the nose. Together, taste and smell do more than make eating pleasant. Stimulation of receptors in the nose and mouth triggers the release of the hormone insulin from the pancreas into the blood. Insulin regulates the body's use of sugar.

Taste is also important to survival. Pleasant tastes stimulate eating behavior so that the body's needs for energy and materials are met. Tastes also signal danger. Nearly all natural poisons taste bitter.

Learning, not biology, dictates food preferences. Writes psychologist Bernard Lyman: "Generally, foods that are liked are ones that have been eaten and found pleasant, but foods may be disliked whether or not they have been tasted."[11] Lyman defines five classes of disliked foods:

You can dislike a food because . . .	For example . . .
you have negative ideas about it, even though you've never tried it.	in our culture, eating caterpillars or worms
its taste or texture was unpleasant when you tried it (but it might have been pleasant if prepared differently).	cooked cabbage versus cole slaw
it becomes boring or overly familiar, especially when someone else controls the menu.	canned peaches daily in the school cafeteria
it causes an allergic reaction.	ice cream can give you stomach pains.
you become ill after eating a food and the association stays with you forever.	you get sick at the carnival and can't stand the sight of cotton candy ever again.

Lyman says the sensory qualities of foods are relatively unimportant. Children dislike foods they have never tried. Characteristics that are pleasant in other foods (for example, salty, crunchy) are rejected in a particular food (deep-fried and salted grasshoppers). Changes in food preferences go along with growing up. Many children don't like hot chilies, but those who grow up in Mexico eventually acquire the taste. Lyman says that culture, emotion, situation, and associations are the true determinants of food preferences.

What Causes Hunger?

You feel hunger in the stomach, but it arises first in the brain. Falling levels of glucose in the blood stimulate the hypothalamus in the brain's limbic system. Nerve impulses from the brain cause the muscular wall of the stomach to contract. As fluid and air pass into the intestine, your stomach "growls." As you eat, the stomach expands. Its expansion sends signals to the brain. It takes about 20 minutes for the signals to reach the brain and register as a feeling of fullness—and for the brain's "satiety centers" to respond by turning off hunger. That's why you may eat more than you really want or need if you eat too fast.

What Makes a Food a "Comfort" Food?

If you associate certain foods with feelings of happiness and security, you are not alone. In her 1943 classic *The Gastronomical Me*, food philosopher M. F. K. Fisher wrote: "It seems to me that our three basic needs, for food and security and love, are so mixed and mingled and entwined that we cannot straightly think of one without the others. So it happens that when I write of hunger, I am really writing about love and the hunger for it, and warmth and the love of it and the hunger for it . . . and then the warmth and richness and fine reality of hunger satisfied . . . and it is all one."[12]

Are Belching, Barping, and Passing Gas Normal? Yes, although you may stay on better terms with your family and friends if you try to exercise some control over when, where, and how loudly you indulge.

Belching and burping usually come from swallowing air when you eat. Stress and anxiety can also cause you to swallow air and belch. So can eating rapidly, drinking fizzy sodas, or taking antacids. To get an idea how antacids release gas, add a little baking soda to some vinegar. That fizz is the carbon-dioxide gas released as the base (the soda) neutralizes the acid (the vinegar). The bubbles are carbon-dioxide gas. The same thing happens in your stomach.

Gas lower down has a different origin. It forms in the large intestine as bacteria break down wastes there. Their chemical activities release hydrogen, methane, and carbon-dioxide gases that have no odor, and hydrogen sulfide that does have an odor.

As Soon as I Eat Breakfast, I Need to Go to the Bathroom. Why? Because your digestive system has a mind of its own—literally!

The enteric nervous system (ENS) functions without direction from the brain. Nerve impulses that originate in the digestive tube trigger the action of hormone-secreting cells. They control the ebb and flow of the blood supply to the gut. The ENS also regulates the contraction of the smooth muscles of the stomach and intestine. The ENS works the same way as the nervous system anywhere else in the body. Messages pass from one nerve cell to another by way of chemicals called neurotransmitters. The ENS uses many of the same ones as the brain. Particularly important are serotonin, which stimulates muscle contraction, and norepinephrine, which slows it.

When food enters the stomach, the ENS neurotransmitters swing into action, producing the gastrocolic reflex. (Reflexes are nervous-system responses that require no command from the brain.) The food stimulates a rise in serotonin. Increased serotonin makes the muscles of the stomach and small intestine squeeze harder than those farther down the tube do. The contractions move food and (later) waste materials in a single direction. The muscle contraction also sends a signal to the brain, directing the appropriate behavioral response. Later, when the stomach empties, serotonin production declines, and the norepinephrine level rises. That calms intestinal contractions until the next meal.

The quantity of food, its temperature, and the amount of energy it contains affect the gastrocolic reflex. That's why a big, hot breakfast of bacon and eggs may send you running for the bathroom faster than a small bowl of cold cereal.

What Causes a Beer Belly?

A double-layered membrane called the greater omentum drapes the small intestine. It prevents infections in the abdominal cavity. It's also a major storage area for fat reserves. Beer isn't the only food that causes fat to accumulate in the greater omentum. Any excess consumption of food energy triggers fat storage in the greater omentum.

If I Need
Energy All the
Time, Why
Don't I Have to
Eat All the
Time?

The liver takes excess glucose from the blood and changes it into a storable form called glycogen. The liver also changes excess amino acids into fats, glucose, or glycogen. When blood-sugar levels fall, because you haven't eaten for a few hours, the pancreas releases glucagon, a hormone that acts on glycogen stored in the liver and in the muscles. It causes the glycogen to break apart into glucose molecules. They enter the bloodstream and raise blood-glucose levels, just as they do after a meal. If glycogen reserves are low, energy comes from stored fat. The conversion of fats to glucose takes longer than the break down of glycogen.

Math ... By Mouth

. . . .

I am convinced digestion is the great secret of life.

SYDNEY SMITH

. . . .

The formulas seem simple enough. If the body takes in more energy than it burns, it stores the excess. That's weight gain. If the body takes in less energy than it uses, it draws on its reserves. That's weight loss. When energy in equals energy out, weight stays the same.

But, as millions of struggling weight watchers and body builders can attest, the mechanisms that control appetite, eating behavior, muscle building, and fat storage are far from simple. The formula *energy out = energy in +/- energy stored* is affected by many complex and interacting variables that scientists are only beginning to understand.

Hormones manufactured in several different organs affect the equation. The pancreas, for example, makes insulin. Insulin is a remarkable hormone. It regulates more processes than does any other. One of its effects is moving glucose out of the blood and into body cells. It also works in the brain to turn off appetite for fats and carbohydrates. In laboratory animals (and perhaps humans), the absence of insulin causes the hypothalamus, a gland in the brain, to produce increased amounts of the protein galanin. Galanin increases appetite and causes cells to decrease their energy use. Rats that do not make insulin have galanin levels 50 percent greater than normal rats.

Galanin isn't the only appetite/energy regulator produced in the hypothalamus. Some others we know about include neuropeptide Y (NPY), which stimulates feeding behavior. Its amounts rise and fall in response to yet another substance, leptin. Leptin is made by fat cells throughout the body and released into the blood. The more stored fat, the more leptin.

When all is in balance, increased leptin leads to decreased NPY production and reduced appetite. That is, when sufficient fat is stored, feeding behavior diminishes. Conversely, when leptin levels drop, NPY production increases. That is, a low fat reserve increases appetite.

If this were the only control mechanism, the 54 percent of Americans who are overweight and the 19 percent now classified as obese might solve their problem

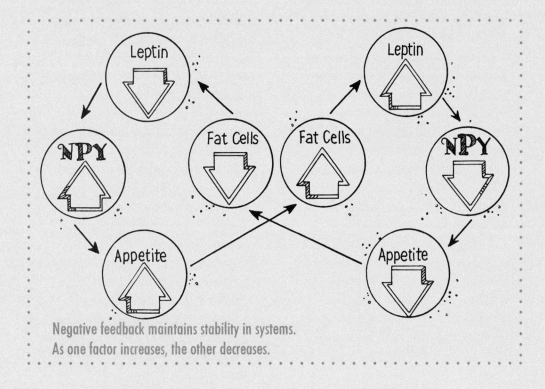

Negative feedback maintains stability in systems. As one factor increases, the other decreases.

easily.[13] They could pop a leptin pill and watch their excess weight fade away. Conversely, wrestlers, weight lifters, and football players trying to "bulk up" might rely on NPY. But, wouldn't you know it, neither "quick fix" works. One reason is that the body adjusts. If leptin levels rise and stay high, leptin resistance develops. It stops affecting NPY production.

Another reason is that many other factors and control pathways are part of the equation. Scientists study specially bred "knockout" mice to find out how they work. ("Knockout" means that a gene has been eliminated or inactivated, so that the animals do not make a particular protein.) One strain of knockout mice lacks the gene for a receptor on cell membranes called Mc3r. Mc3r binds to α-MSH (for alpha melanocyte stimulating hormone). The brain produces this hormone in response to leptin.

Mice lacking the Mc3r receptor appear to grow normally until they are 26 weeks old. Their average weight is no different, but they actually have 50 to 60 percent more fat in their bodies than mice that have Mc3r receptors.[14] As the knockout mice age, their appearance changes. They eat less, but they gain more weight per calorie of food consumed. Their body temperature, thyroid function, and rate of fuel burning are all normal. They are, however, about half as active. They also produce less NPY, which may explain their reduced food intake.

Another, similar receptor is Mc4r. Researchers have studied knockout mice lacking these receptors. The knockout mice eat more than normal mice and become obese. Their lean body weight is the same as normal mice, but they burn calories at a lower rate. Mice lacking both Mc3r and Mc4r gain more weight than either of the single knockout types. They eat more and store fat more efficiently.

What's true in mice may not be true in humans, but genes and receptors aren't the only influences. Another may be viral infections. Investigators at the University of Wisconsin at Madison have studied the human adenovirus-36, nicknamed Ad-36. It causes mild, coldlike symptoms in people. When they injected it into chickens, the birds stored 60 to 75 percent more fat than uninfected controls.[15] The experimental chickens didn't eat any more, but the infection reduced their activity. "Chickens who get the virus sit in a lump all day long," says researcher Nikhil Dhurandhar, instead of scratching and pecking like healthy birds.[16] Is this a general response to any viral infection? No. Only Ad-36 does it.[17] Does this mean obesity is contagious? No. The virus is gone long before effects appear.

Australian researchers have studied a strain of rats bred to mimic humans in their patterns of obesity. *Psammonys obesus* individuals vary as much as humans do. Most maintain a moderate weight and body fat content, but some grow obese while others stay thin. The rats' appetites vary in the same way. Some eat more than others when given free access to a standard laboratory diet.

The researchers isolated a gene in *P. obesus* that causes the hypothalamus to make a small protein called beacon. The greater the amount of beacon made in the hypothalamus, the greater the percentage of body fat the animal

stores. When the scientists infused more beacon into their brains, the rats ate more and gained weight. The effect was "dose dependent." The more beacon they received, the more food they consumed and the more energy they stored. When beacon and NPY were given together, the increases were even more dramatic. The amount of weight gained was greater than could be explained by increased food consumption.

Meanwhile, scientists in Massachusetts were isolating a protein that controls body weight in mice without affecting their food intake. Fat cells make the protein, called Acrp30. When researchers gave a fragment of Acrp30 to mice, the animals didn't gain weight, even on a high-fat diet. Chubby mice lost weight and levels of fatty acids in their blood declined. It appears that Acrp30 circulates in the blood and causes muscles to burn fatty acids more rapidly.

As promising as this research is, it does not change the basic energy equation for the millions of people who want to gain or lose weight. The only variables under conscious control remain energy in (food) and energy out (exercise).

· · · ·

CHAPTER TWO

ABOUT FOOD AND GOOD HEALTH

To eat is human, to digest divine.

• CHARLES T. COPELAND •

What Do Vitamins Do?
Like carbohydrates, fats, and proteins, vitamins are carbon-based molecules. However, the body does not break them down and use them for energy. Instead, vitamins maintain their structure. They pass into the blood and body cells with their form intact. There, they act in many different ways to:

- **regulate chemical reactions:** *Example:* Pyridoxine (a form of vitamin B$_6$), works along with enzymes that break down amino acids.

- **promote absorption, exchange, and storage of materials:** *Example:* Vitamin D enhances the absorption of calcium from food.

Without it, the body pulls calcium from the bones to supply the daily needs of nerves and muscles.

- **contribute to life processes:** *Example:* Folic acid is needed to make the genetic material, DNA. Without it, DNA cannot copy itself, and cells do not divide.

- **form cell structures:** *Example:* Vitamin C forms part of the protein collagen that gives skin its strength and elasticity.

The body can make some vitamins, but most must be obtained from food. Many different vitamins are known. Some are named for letters of the alphabet. Each has a distinct chemical structure. Each performs a different job in the body, and many have several functions. To learn more, see Table 1 on page 142-145.

What Minerals Must I Get From Food, and Why Do I Need Them?

Minerals are inorganic (meaning "not carbon") elements that are used in many of the body's structures and processes. Some minerals enter the body only as parts of something else. For example, cobalt forms part of vitamin B_{12}, and the amino acids methionine and cystine in protein foods contain sulfur.

Some of the minerals that humans must get from food or water include the following:

- **calcium,** which builds teeth and bones. It is needed for nerve impulses to travel, blood to clot, and muscles to contract. Many enzymes need calcium to work properly.

- **chlorine**, which is part of stomach acid. It is used in transporting the waste material, carbon-dioxide gas, from body cells to the lungs.

- **iron**, which forms part of hemoglobin, the compound in red blood cells that carries oxygen. Iron gives blood its color.

- **potassium**, which helps maintain the body's water and acid-base balances. The exchange of sodium and potassium across membranes carries nerve impulses.

- **selenium**, which breaks down the destructive waste material hydrogen peroxide in cells. It protects the membranes of cells and mitochondria from oxidation damage. It may also tie up poisonous heavy metals such as mercury and reduce their toxicity.

- **fluorine**, which becomes part of teeth and bones.

- **iodine**, which is used in the thyroid gland in making hormones. The hormones regulate the body's rate of oxygen consumption and energy use.

- **magnesium**, which contributes to energy release, protein manufacture, the activities of nerves and muscles, and the formation of urea (the main waste in urine). It also binds to calcium and protects tooth enamel against decay.

- **chromium**, which is involved in carbohydrate metabolism. It may play a role in binding insulin to cell membranes.

- **zinc**, which affects production of a hormone in the thymus gland called Th-1. Th-1 plays a part in the manufacture of "natural killer" cells, an important weapon of the immune system in its battle against infections and cancer cells.

For more information on specific minerals, see Table 2 on page 146-149.

How Do Vitamins and Minerals Prevent Disease? Many mechanisms are possible. One of the most widely researched is the action of the antioxidant vitamins such as A, C, and E. Antioxidants prevent or repair the damage that free radicals inflict on cells. Free radicals are atoms or molecules that contain oxygen in a highly reactive form. They are the same kinds of compounds that cause iron to rust, stone to crumble, and paint to peel. In cells, free radicals steal electrons (negatively charged particles that orbit the nuclei of atoms) from other compounds, causing them to break down in structure and fail in function. Their action injures cell membranes, alters DNA, and interferes with life-sustaining chemical reactions. Vitamins aren't the only antioxidants in cells, but all seem to act in a similar manner—preventing or repairing the damage done by free radicals.

How Much of a Vitamin or Mineral Is Enough? Read the label on a multiple vitamin/mineral supplement at the drugstore. You'll see that most express their contents as a percent of the daily value recommended by the government. The suggested amounts are based on research. However, some requirements are unknown, and new research can cause recommendations to change.

Food scientists use IUs (international units) to measure vitamins A and D. (40 IU = 1 microgram, or 0.000001 gram.) They express vitamin B_{12} needs in micrograms (mcg) and B_6 requirements in milligrams (1mg = 0.001 gram). If those numbers boggle your mind, don't worry. Just choose foods such as those suggested in the table below, and you'll meet or exceed your daily requirements for the nutrients listed.

FOODS (examples)	DAILY NEED (ages 11-18)
2 fresh apricots + 1 tomato + 1 avocado	Vitamin A (4,000 IU for females—5,000 IU for males)
3 oz. salmon	Vitamin B_{12} (1.8 mg for younger—2.4 mg for older)
1 cup romaine lettuce + ½ cup asparagus + 6 oz. orange juice + 1 oz. peanuts + ½ cup kidney beans	Folate (300 mcg for males—400 mcg for females)
2 medium kiwis or 1 cup red bell pepper or ½ cantaloupe	Vitamin C (60 mg for younger—90 mg for older)
1 cup skim milk + 2 Eggo waffles + ½ cup low-fat frozen yogurt	Calcium (1,300 mg)
1 baked potato + ½ cup cooked spinach + 3 oz. lean beef + 3 spears broccoli	Iron (12 mg for males—15 mg for females)
¾ cup bran cereal + ½ cup tuna + ½ cup lima beans	Zinc (12 mg for females—15 mg for males)
1 Brazil nut	Selenium (40 mcg for younger—50 mcg for older)

Should I Take a Multiple Vitamin and Mineral Pill Every day?

Ask your doctor or a registered dietitian. Many say yes, but not as a substitute for a poor diet. "Real foods contain the nutrients we know about and many more that we do not," says neuroscientist Eric Chudler."[1]

Research is often done with supplements, because investigators can control doses and timing more easily with supplements than they can with whole foods. In many cases, supplements show benefits. In others, however, they fail when compared with real foods and may even pose hazards of their own. For example, some studies suggest that vitamin A supplements actually increase the risk for some cancers, while foods rich in vitamin A are known to reduce it.[2]

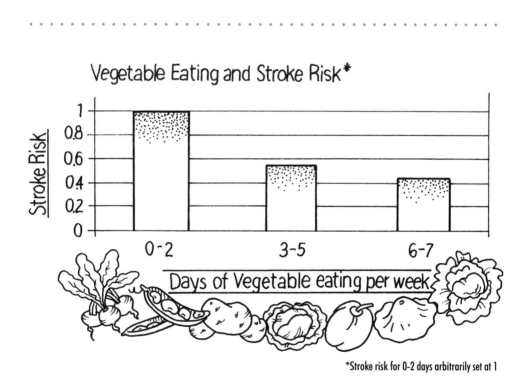

Vegetable Eating and Stroke Risk*

*Stroke risk for 0-2 days arbitrarily set at 1

The more days per week that vegetables are consumed, the lower the risk of stroke.

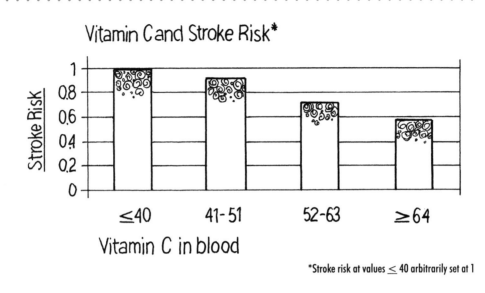

Vitamin C and Stroke Risk*

Stroke Risk

1
0.8
0.6
0.4
0.2
0

≤40   41-51   52-63   ≥64

Vitamin C in blood

*Stroke risk at values ≤ 40 arbitrarily set at 1

Greater amounts of vitamin C in the blood are associated with reduced risk of stroke.

Studies of vitamin C produced similar results. Researchers in Japan studied vitamin C and stroke risk in more than 2,000 people for a full 20 years! Hardly any of the people took vitamin pills, but many ate v egetable-rich diets. The results were dramatic. Those who ate vegetables often and had the highest levels of vitamin C in their blood cut their risk of stroke by 40 to 60 percent.[3]

So it would make sense that taking vitamin C pills would have the same effect. To test that idea, researchers studied the risk of stroke in men who took extra doses of vitamin C. The results were disappointing. The supplements didn't affect stroke risks greatly.[4] "There is no substitute for the rich mix of raw materials that whole foods provide," Chudler says.[5]

Cholesterol has a worse reputation than it deserves. This waxy lipid (a kind of fat) is essential to good health. It builds the membranes that hold cells together. It's used in making certain hormones and the digestive fluid, bile. It's also part of the protective covering that wraps nerve fibers.

Cholesterol is only bad when it forms plaques that block arteries and impede blood flow. If the supply of blood to the heart is blocked, a person develops heart disease and faces the risk of a heart attack. If cholesterol blocks the blood supply to the brain, a stroke may result.

The cholesterol molecule does not dissolve in the liquid portion of the blood. Instead, it circulates attached to water-soluble compounds called lipoproteins. High-density lipoproteins, HDLs, are the "good" carriers. They transport cholesterol away from artery walls to the liver for disposal. They also prevent free radicals from combining with oxygen and damaging artery walls.

Low-density lipoproteins, or LDLs, are the "bad" carriers. The cholesterol is no different—only the molecule it rides on. LDLs are "bad" because they carry cholesterol all around the body. They let it attach to artery walls. If it combines with oxygen there, it attracts white blood cells to the site. The body treats a buildup of oxidized LDL-cholesterol as an injury. The area becomes inflamed, then heals, only to become inflamed and heal again. That sets the stage for a blood clot or heart attack.

Only about 20 percent of the body's cholesterol comes from animal foods, such as meat, milk, eggs, and butter.[6] The liver makes the rest from materials obtained from fatty foods. Limiting fat in the diet helps reduce LDLs. Limiting amounts of luncheon meats, fatty beef, poultry skin, candy, bakery treats, fried foods, and whole-milk products such as butter and cheese is a good idea for most teens and adults. For most people older than age two, low-fat substitutes—such as skim milk for whole milk—are a good idea. (Fat intake should not be restricted before the age of two, because fat is important for the formation of myelin, the protective sheath that surrounds nerves.) Nutritionists also recommend using liquid vegetable oils and soft spreads instead of hard margarine.

What Is Fiber, and Why Do I Need It? Fiber is a broad term for certain large, stable carbohydrate molecules in plant foods that humans can't digest. They include the cellulose from plant cell walls and pectin, the plant material that causes jelly to set. The richest sources of fiber are whole-grain breads and cereals, beans, vegetables, nuts, and fruits.

Fiber adds bulk to feces, making it softer and easier to eliminate. Fiber may also decrease the time that it takes for feces to pass through the large intestine. Some experts believe that faster transit reduces opportunities for cancer-causing substances to form and be absorbed. That idea may explain why many studies (but not all) show that fiber-rich diets—especially those high in fiber from fruits and vegetables—help prevent colon cancer.

Fiber decreases cholesterol in the blood, perhaps by reducing the amount absorbed from food. Oats, barley, rye, and other whole grains deserve their reputation as cholesterol-busters. They are high in fiber. Four to six servings daily of citrus fruits (especially their white inner rind), apples, berries, carrots, dates, figs, prunes, cabbage, brussels sprouts, beans, lentils, peas, or sweet potatoes can lower cholesterol levels by as much as 10 percent.[7] Numerous studies show a whopping 40 to 50 percent reduction in the risk of heart disease and stroke associated with high fiber intake.[8] Fiber may also play a role in preventing and controlling diabetes.

What's So Bad About Fast Food?

The trouble with fast food is that it makes every day not one feast day, but two.

Think back to last Thanksgiving. Did you, like many Americans, eat the standard servings of turkey, stuffing, creamed vegetables, salad, mashed potatoes, a roll, and pumpkin pie? If you did, you took in about 1,900 calories in food energy and about 83 grams of fat. That's nearly an entire day's energy supply obtained in just one meal. Your Thanksgiving dinner got 38 percent of its energy from fat. That's higher than the recommended 25–30 percent, but Thanksgiving comes only once a year. The fat and calories should average out with a more modest food intake on other days. Right?

Maybe not. Consider a busy school day or workday when fast food is the easiest, quickest, and tastiest choice available. For breakfast, you swing through the drive-in for a muffin with egg and sausage, a cinnamon roll (to save for your mid-morning break), and orange juice. Lunch is a quick burger, large fries, and a small shake. At dinner, takeout beckons. You pick up chicken nuggets with honey mustard sauce, a chef's salad with croutons and Caesar dressing, a baked apple pie, and a large cola.

Not an unusual day for many Americans, but how does this day compare with Thanksgiving? At 3,900 calories and 172 grams of fat, it's not one Thanksgiving feast, but more than two! What's more, your traditional Thanksgiving dinner delivered vitamins and minerals that fast food cannot match.[9]

The American Societies for Nutritional Science and Clinical Nutrition define junk foods as those that don't fit into any of the five major food groups: dairy, fruit, grains, meat and beans, or vegetables. One-third of the average American diet falls into the junk-food categories.[10] These include:

- fats such as butter, oil, salad dressings, gravy

- sweeteners such as sugar, syrup, candy, sugar-sweetened soft drinks

- desserts such as cookies, cakes, pastries, ice cream, pudding

- salty snacks such as potato chips or tortilla chips

- miscellaneous items such as coffee, tea, and alcohol

Not all fast food is junk food. A hamburger patty is meat, and the bun is bread. The cheese on a pizza is a dairy product, and its tomato-based sauce belongs in the fruit-and-vegetable category. However, the fat in fast foods often propels them into the junk-food category. Fast-food french fries contain more fat than potatoes.

A cup of soup sounds like a good idea for lunch. You pull two cans from the shelf. One is chili. The other is potato soup with meat and cheese.

The labels show that the chili contains 290 calories of energy per cup; the soup, 200. Either one is all right, you think, considering that you need about 2,000 to 2,500 calories a day, and you're feeling mighty hungry.

Nutrition Facts		
Serv Size 1 cup (242g)		
Servings about 2		
Amount Per Serving		
Calories 290	Fat cal 120	
		% Daily Value*
Total Fat 14g		22%
Sat Fat 5g		25%
Cholest. 40mg		13%
Sodium 930mg		39%
Total Carb. 29g		10%
Fiber 10g		40%
Sugars 2g		
Protein 20g		
Vitamin A 4% • Vitamin C 8%		
Calcium 10% • Iron 25%		

Chili label

Nutrition Facts		
Serving Size 1 cup (240mL)		
Servings Per Container about 2		
Amount Per Serving		
Calories 200	Calories from Fat 80	
		% Daily Value*
Total Fat 9g		14%
Saturated Fat 3.5g		18%
Cholesterol 20mg		7%
Sodium 970mg		40%
Total Carbohydrate 21g		7%
Dietary Fiber 2g		8%
Sugars 2g		
Protein 8g		
Vitamin A 4% • Vitamin C 6%		
Calcium 4% • Iron 6%		

*Percent Daily Values are based on a 2,000 calorie diet. Your daily values may be higher or lower depending on your calorie needs:

	Calories:	2,000	2,500
Total Fat	Less than	65g	80g
Sat Fat	Less than	20g	25g
Cholesterol	Less than	300mg	300mg
Sodium	Less than	2,400mg	2,400mg
Total Carbohydrate		300g	375g
Dietary Fiber		25g	30g

Soup label

But what about the other numbers? You know fiber in your diet is healthy. The label says the chili contains 10 grams. That's 40 percent of your daily requirement. That's pretty good, you think, but the chili also delivers 14 grams of fat, 5 of them as the saturated fats that experts suggest you limit. Considering the fat, maybe the potato soup is a better choice.

Both the chili and the soup provide some important vitamins and minerals, but the chili equals or exceeds the soup on the four listed: vitamin A, calcium, vitamin C, and iron. Both, unfortunately, are too salty. They deliver in a single cup nearly half of the sodium your body needs in a day. Although many people can get by with excess salt, those with a family history of high blood pressure may want to steer clear.

So which do you choose? For most people, the answer is either one. As long as breakfast and dinner aren't too high in fat, the chili is okay. And as long as other foods in the diet provide more fiber (such as the salad, whole-grain roll, and fruit you can have with lunch), the soup is okay, too. The keys are variety and quantity. Choosing chili today and potato soup tomorrow balances some of the negatives and positives of each. So does paying attention to portion size. Notice that these cans contain not one serving, but two.

What about foods that aren't labeled? Nutritional information about meats, fruits, and vegetables is displayed in grocery stores. Nutritional handbooks are available in most libraries. The government does not require labels on foods sold in cafeterias, on airplanes, and by street vendors. Bakeries, delis, and candy stores need not provide nutritional information either, although some do. As for fast-food restaurants, look for a wall poster, ask for a brochure, or go online to the company's Web site.

What's So Bad About Sugar in Food? Nothing, in and of itself. Sugar (glucose) is the body's basic fuel. You couldn't survive without it. The trouble lies in the form and quantity of sugar consumed. Fruit and milk have small amounts of natural sugar in them. They also provide other important vitamins and minerals. Carbonated drinks, lemonade, candy, cookies, cake, and ice cream contain a lot of sugar. However, they provide few, if any, other nutrients. These "empty calories" can displace other, more nutritious foods from the diet.

The average American consumes 68.5 pounds (31 kilograms) of sugar a year. That's up 28 percent since 1982.[11] Experts think that's too much,

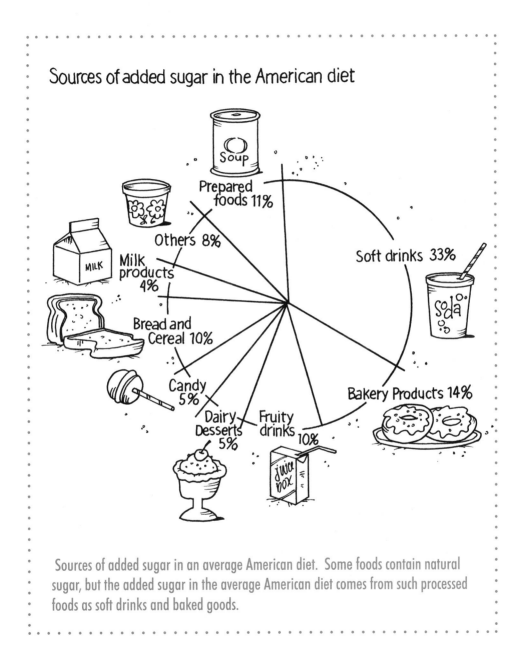

Sources of added sugar in the American diet

Prepared foods 11%

Others 8%

Milk products 4%

Bread and Cereal 10%

Candy 5%

Dairy Desserts 5%

Fruity drinks 10%

Soft drinks 33%

Bakery Products 14%

Sources of added sugar in an average American diet. Some foods contain natural sugar, but the added sugar in the average American diet comes from such processed foods as soft drinks and baked goods.

not because the sugar itself is harmful, but because those who eat the most sugar eat less of other, healthier foods. In one study, people who ate the most sugar got the least of vitamins A, C, B_{12}, and folate and the minerals calcium, phosphorus, magnesium, zinc, and iron. They also took in more energy—perhaps more than they expended.

If you want to cut back on sugar, you'll need to do more than hide the sugar bowl. "It's important for consumers to recognize that they get large amounts of added sugars through processed foods and beverages," says Shanthy Bowman of the U.S. Department of Agriculture.[12] Check the ingredient lists on prepared foods, such as the labels on page 49. You might not expect sugar in potato soup or chili, but it's there— under such names as sucrose, dextrose, modified food starch, and corn syrup.

Should I Eat Butter or Margarine?

Save the wonderful taste of butter for an occasional treat, and eat soft margarine in small amounts.

Butter and margarine have the same calorie and fat content, but they differ in the kinds of fats they contain. Both contain substances that pose health risks. The *saturated* fats in meats, full-fat dairy products, and butter raise cholesterol levels. The hardening of vegetable oils into margarine creates *trans-fatty acids*, which reduce blood-vessel function and lower levels of the good cholesterol.[13] The American Heart Association recommends margarine instead of butter. The organization advises shopping for the soft varieties that are lower in trans-fatty acids. The best ones list liquid vegetable oil as their first ingredient on the label.

"It's healthy . . . cool . . . and has the potential to drive your parents nuts. Three times a day," writes Stephanie Pierson in *Vegetables Rock! A Complete Guide for Teenage Vegetarians*. Only you can decide to fight that battle, and you may do it for reasons that have little to do with nutrition. If you do, rest assured: You need not eat meat to be healthy. In fact, most of us would be healthier if we ate less of it. Nevertheless, a plant-based diet of chips, soft drinks, and cupcakes won't meet the body's needs. The keys to a healthy vegetarian diet are variety and keeping an eye on fats and sugars.

Variety ensures that the body's need for all the essential amino acids are met. Soy is a complete protein. It contains all the essential amino acids. Most other single plant foods don't, but when several are included in the diet, they complement one another. For example, whole grains are good protein sources, but they are missing the amino acid lysine. A diet that relied on grains alone for protein would result in a lysine deficiency. A diet that combines grains with beans, peas, nuts, and tofu (soy) delivers the missing lysine.

Variety also takes care of most vitamin and mineral needs. The iron found in plants is not as easily absorbed by the body as that in animal foods, but the vitamin C in fruits and vegetables aids absorption from breads and cereals, lentils, soy products, and oatmeal. The body's need for calcium can be met with soy milk (often fortified with calcium) and beans. Dark-green, leafy vegetables contain calcium, too, although the body can't absorb it as well as it does the calcium in dairy products. Spending some time in the sun (using a sunscreen to protect the skin against ultraviolet damage) takes care of vitamin D requirements. The only nutritional need that can't be met with plant foods alone is vitamin

B_{12}. It is essential to the formation of red blood cells and the health of the nervous system. Long-term vegetarians should talk with a doctor or nutritionist about taking B_{12} supplements.

Many people who decide to become vegetarians are surprised that they need to watch the level of fats in their diets, but it's true—especially for ovo-lacto vegetarians who eat eggs and cheese. These are high-fat foods, as are salad dressing, nuts, avocados, fried potatoes, and such bakery delights as vegetarian doughnuts, pies, and cookies. Margarines made from vegetable oils are 100 percent fat. That's the same as butter made from cow's milk. Sugar levels can be high in many plant-based foods, too. Apple juice sounds healthier than it is, mostly because its sugar content is high. So are many meal-replacement bars and "power snacks" sold as vegetarian. Too much fatty, sugary foods can push an otherwise healthy vegetarian diet into the same high risks for cancer and heart disease that meat-eaters face.

Everybody Says I Should Drink a Lot of Water, But Nobody Says Why. Is There a Reason?

Try three: **1. Survival.** About two-thirds of your body weight is water.[14] All the body's chemical reactions occur in water, and you can survive—at best—three to five days without it. Most of the body's water comes from drinks and foods, but water produced as a by-product of metabolism provides some, too. The body loses water in urine, feces, sweat, and breath.

2. The Feel-Good Factor. Some experts say that too little water can make you tired. Elizabeth Somer, author of *Food and Mood,* recommends six to eight glasses a day.[15] Without enough water, she says, blood flows sluggishly, diminishing the supply of nutrients to the brain.

Soft drinks are no substitute. They cause the kidneys to excrete more water into the urine, not less.

3. Disease Prevention. Water prevents kidney stones by keeping the urine diluted. Kidney stones are lumps of minerals and carbon compounds that form in the kidneys. The more concentrated the urine, the more likely that kidney stones will form. A stone begins around a clump of bacteria, some dead cells, or a tiny blood clot. Minerals in the urine collect on it and encrust it. If kidney stones get large, they can interfere with the production and elimination of urine. They are also extremely painful. Drinking lots of water helps flush out minerals and tiny stones before they can grow.

Do I Really Have to Drink Milk? Yes, and lots of it, or enjoy other calcium-rich foods such as yogurt, low-fat cheese, dark leafy green vegetables, and broccoli. There are two reasons. One is the present. The other is the future.

The "here and now" need is for calcium to support bone growth, muscle contraction, strong teeth, and a healthy nervous system. A deficiency of calcium in the diet—or a failure of the body to absorb it—can cause confusion and memory loss, seizures, breathing difficulties, and abnormal heart rhythms.

The future consideration is to have bones strong enough to last a lifetime. If the blood contains too little calcium to support muscle action and nerve function, it pulls the calcium from the bones. That action can lead to osteoporosis—a condition of weak, brittle bones that break easily. It affects more than 10 million Americans.[16] Most of them are female, and women over age 50 face a 50:50 risk of a bone fracture related to osteoporosis at some time in their lives.[17] By age 65, men lose

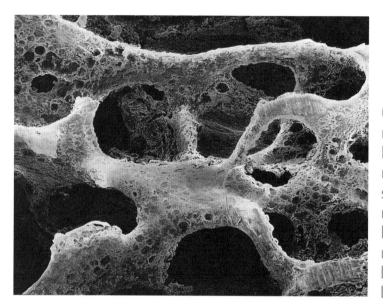

bone mass as fast as women do, and by age 75, one-third of men have osteoporosis.[18] That makes building strong bones early in life extremely important for both sexes. Getting plenty of calcium in food, along with the vitamin D that helps the digestive system to absorb it, seems to retard (but not totally prevent) the disease.

Exercise is also important, especially in the teens and twenties when bone formation is greatest. "The key is to achieve a peak bone density during the time in your life when your body is building your skeleton," says Thomas Einhorn, professor of orthopedics and director of orthopedic research at New York's Mount Sinai Hospital. "You've only got until about age 25 to do that," he adds.[19] Einhorn recommends dancing, walking, running, and aerobics to stimulate bone-cell activity, thus increasing bone density and strength. Weight lifting does the same for the bones of the upper body.

"People who eat at least five daily servings of fruits and vegetables reduce their cancer incidence by as much as twenty percent," says Melanie Polk, director of nutrition education at the American Institute for Cancer Research. Of the 247 studies the Institute reviewed, 80 percent showed that plant foods protect cells from cancer-causing agents. They also slow the growth and spread of cancerous tumors.[20]

Several factors may explain such benefits. Vegetables contain a mixture of beneficial substances, including large amounts of vitamins such as folic acid and minerals such as potassium. The bright-colored vegetables have pigments called carotenoids that act as antioxidants. One carotenoid is lutein. It may help prevent colon cancer and macular degeneration, the major cause of blindness among the elderly. Lutein is plentiful in spinach, kale, oranges, broccoli, carrots, and celery.

The benefits of fruits and vegetables cannot be traced to a single factor, however, but to a combination. "Growing evidence suggests that it is the range of agents in fruits and vegetables that together may offer the observed protection," says Graham Colditz, an epidemiologist at Harvard Medical School.[21]

Cancer prevention isn't the only health benefit of vegetables. They reduce the risk of stroke (see graph, page 43), diabetes, heart disease, and the other major killing and crippling diseases. "Get your daily five," is good advice for everyone.

Cravings are common, and they have nothing to do with hunger. Hunger, the actual need for food, comes with intestinal rumblings, stomach pangs, and sometimes a headache. Almost any food will satisfy it. Cravings are different. They are the desire for a single food, and they cannot be dispelled with a substitute.

Most people crave a particular food from time to time. Harvey Weingarten at McMaster University in Hamilton, Ontario, surveyed 1,000 undergraduates. Among women, 97 percent reported craving specific foods—most often chocolate, with other sweet treats such as cookies, cake, candy, and ice cream close behind. Two-thirds of the men admitted craving specific foods—sometimes chocolate, but more often high-protein or high-fat foods such as meat or lasagna. Both men and women said they experienced cravings between five and nine times a month.[22]

Cravings are often associated with stress. Stress, some experts say, provokes release of the hormone cortisol. Cortisol brings on a craving for carbohydrates. Carbohydrate foods cause the brain to make more of the neurotransmitter serotonin. Serotonin delivers feelings of relaxation and contentment. Endorphins, the morphinelike neurotransmitters in the brain that ease pain, soothe stress, and produce feelings of pleasure, are also powerful craving inducers.

Forget, however, the myth that the body craves foods that contain nutrients it needs. If that were true, you'd crave foods such as kale and beans—and hardly anyone does. Many people crave salty foods, although most of us get more salt in our diets than we need. "No research has associated low vitamin intakes with a craving for a food rich in that nutrient," says food expert Catherine Christie.[23]

Do I Have to Eat Breakfast?

Consider these facts, then decide:

• In Maryland, students who ate breakfast improved their test scores by 11 percent over students who didn't.[24]

- In Massachusetts, breakfast-eating students improved their test scores and reduced rates of tardiness and absenteeism.

- A University of Iowa study showed that students who skipped breakfast had trouble concentrating in school and became restless by late morning. Eating breakfast prevents irritability and fatigue, says the International Food Information Council.

- Breakfast helps in weight control. In one study, people who ate cereal for breakfast ate fewer calories from fat throughout the day and consumed 20 percent more essential vitamins and minerals.[25] Breakfast skippers eat more later in the day and are more likely to select energy-dense foods. As a result, breakfast skippers are more likely to become overweight than breakfast eaters.

- A Harvard Medical School study concluded that students who eat breakfast are happier and more energetic. They are less likely to get into arguments with teachers and friends. "Kids who eat breakfast tend to have more strength and endurance, and better concentration and problem-solving ability," says dietitian Althea Zanecosky.[26]

How Do I Know If a Food Is "Good for Me?"

First, let's change the question. No food is bad. It's just that some are better choices more often and in larger quantities than others. It's common sense really. Fried foods, sugar-laden drinks, salty snacks, pies, cookies, creamy desserts, and candies are occasional treats—not everyday staples.

Can Eating Right Make People Live Longer? There are no guarantees, but it appears that healthy eating can improve the chances of long life. Scientists at the National Cancer Institute studied questionnaires completed by 42,000 women. They found that those who ate diets rich in fruits, vegetables, whole grains, and low-fat dairy products reduced their risk of dying from cancer, heart disease, and stroke by 30 percent over a six-year period.[27] No one lives forever, and healthy diet is one factor among many (including exercise and not smoking), but the promise of such substantial benefits does make eating your greens seem more attractive.

Your Friend, the Fat Cell

Food is an important part of a balanced diet.
FRAN LEBOWITZ

I t's not the survival of the fittest, some say, but survival of the fattest. The logic goes like this. Throughout most of human history, famines were the norm. Many people died of starvation. Those whose bodies stored energy most efficiently didn't die. They survived and reproduced, passing on their fat-storing genes to their offspring. Getting fat was an advantage for survival. That's why most of us store fat well (too well?) today.

That theory is debatable, but the basic premise is not. Fat is normal and healthy—to a point. Humans wouldn't survive without it. Fat-storing tissue beneath the skin conserves body heat. It acts as a shock-absorbing pad that protects body organs against injury. Fats contain the body's reserve of vitamins A, D, and E. Some of the substances stored in fat are growth factors. Others are essential for normal sexual development and reproduction.

A healthy, full-grown body contains about 35 billion fat cells. Each contains about 0.5 microgram of fat.[28] How do fat cells form? Researchers at the University of Michigan studied a class of proteins called *Wnt*. These proteins prevent

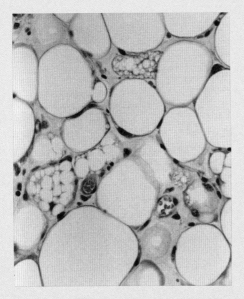

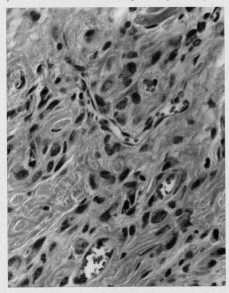

In mice, fat cells (top) fail to form when Wnt proteins halt their development (bottom).

cells from becoming receptacles for fat storage. When *Wnt* is not made, fat cells are free to form. One important area for fat-cell formation is just under the skin. Fat cells also form between the muscles, around the intestines and the membranes that support them, around the heart, and elsewhere. Stored fat comes partly from food and partly from the body's own fat-making activities. Fat is the body's principal energy reserve. It is used during long periods of exertion, such as running a marathon. It is also critical when food is in short supply, a situation that still faces much of the world's population today.

Humans must get at least six essential fatty acids from food, because the body cannot make them. A deficiency of fatty acids reduces the number of blood-clotting cells called platelets, causes fat to collect in the liver, and makes wounds hard to heal. Other symptoms may include scaly skin, poor healing, and diminished hair growth.

Fat-containing foods such as nuts, peanut butter, and olive oil reduce the risk of heart disease. These foods contain plant sterols. The sterols are fatlike substances that interfere with absorption of artery-clogging cholesterol from foods. They also contain monounsaturated fatty acids. Researchers at Penn State University found that people who get their monounsaturated fats from peanut butter reduce their risk of cardiovascular disease by 21 percent.[29]

Among other friends of the fat cell are the oily fish. The omega-3 fatty acids in fish oils lower cholesterol levels. Too few of them in the diet elevate the risks of heart disease, stroke, high blood pressure, rheumatoid arthritis, and inflammatory bowel disease. As few as two servings of salmon, tuna, anchovies, or sardines a week cuts the risk of sudden death from heart disease or stroke. Some plant foods contain another substance, ALA, which the body converts to omega-3 fatty acids. These foods include English walnuts, tofu, and canola oil.

Fat cells are friends, unless they grow too large in size and number. Obese bodies often have twice as many fat cells as bodies of normal weight, and the cells are twice as big.[30] "Obesity is now the most prevalent disease of children and young adults in the U.S.," says

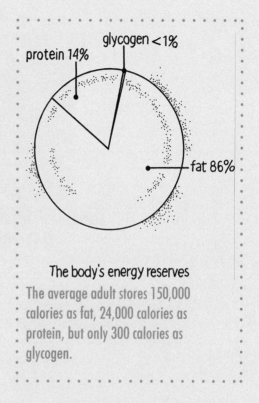

The body's energy reserves
The average adult stores 150,000 calories as fat, 24,000 calories as protein, but only 300 calories as glycogen.

Theresa Nicklas, a public-health expert at the Baylor College of Medicine. Since 1960, obesity has increased 40 percent among people 12 to 17 years old, she reports.[31] Losing weight doesn't decrease the number of fat cells, but it does decrease their size. Fat loss isn't easy, but it's important for those who need it. Obesity is a major risk factor for diabetes, heart disease, high blood pressure, stroke, and cancer.

• • • •

CHAPTER THREE

ABOUT WHEN THINGS GO WRONG

"You'll be sick tomorrow, Jack, if you eat any more chocolates,"
said Sylvia Llewelyn-Davies to her young son. "I shall be sick
tonight," said the child calmly, as he helped himself to another.

• J. M. Barrie •
(who used this true-life conversation
in his classic play *Peter Pan*)

What Makes Me Feel Sick to My Stomach When I Have the Flu?

That feeling of "I'm going to throw up . . . I wish I would," comes from the base of the brain. When your immune system begins fighting a pathogen, it releases into the blood a substance called TNF (for tumor necrosis factor). When TNF reaches the brain stem, it influences the nerve cells there that control digestion. In response to TNF's message, the nerves send signals that slow digestion. Interrupting the digestive process produces nausea.

The impulse to vomit comes not from the gut but from the brain. One region at the base of the brain detects toxins and drugs in the blood. It can stimulate another region, the vomiting center. Or the vomiting center may be stimulated directly by organs responding to disease or stress. In either case, nerve impulses travel from the brain to the stomach and abdominal muscles. They cause the sheet of muscle that lies between the lungs and stomach to push down. The walls of the stomach contract.

The round muscle that lies between the stomach and the duodenum (the pyloric sphincter) closes. The opening between the esophagus and stomach relaxes. Contraction of the abdominal muscles forces food back up through the esophagus and out through the mouth. The expelling food cannot enter the windpipe. The epiglottis closes over the vocal cords (larynx) and blocks entry to the airway. Sometimes, the stomach empties completely, and only bitter-tasting bile comes up. That happens because bile backs up from the duodenum into the stomach.

Drugs, tainted foods, and many illnesses provoke vomiting. It's self-defense. It rids the body of poisons. Motion sickness and seasickness are different. They result from overstimulation of the fluid-filled canals in the inner ear where balance is maintained. Vomiting isn't a serious threat to health unless it is frequent, lasts days, contains blood, or is accompanied by severe pain. Vomit that is red, black, or the consistency of coffee grounds requires immediate medical attention. There may be bleeding in the digestive system.

The usual explanation is that elevated levels of pregnancy hormones in the blood trigger the vomiting center. But evidence casts doubt on that explanation. Pregnant women who throw up have about the same levels of hormones as those who escape the "morning miseries." Morning sickness usually goes away after the first three months of pregnancy, although hormone levels stay high. In societies that eat mostly plant foods, morning sickness is rare. In meat-eating societies, it's common.

So what's going on? One idea is that morning sickness protects the developing embryo. During the early weeks of pregnancy, the baby's major body organs and systems form. At that time, they are especially vulnerable to any poisons the mother might consume. Many women report avoiding animal foods for fear of morning sickness. Animal foods are more likely to spoil and produce toxins than plant foods. Therefore, this notion suggests, morning sickness increases the chance of a healthy pregnancy and a healthy baby.

Studies in countries where women have good nutrition seem to confirm this hypothesis. Women who have morning sickness are less likely to miscarry than those who don't. In poor countries, however, where pregnant women don't always get the good food they need, morning sickness is harmful. Ohio State University researchers studied the Turkana people of Kenya. They found that those mothers who vomited faced double the risk of miscarriage or infant death.[1]

What Is the Appendix, and Why Do So Many People Have Theirs Removed?

The appendix is a small, worm-shaped pocket. It protrudes from the colon near the point where it joins the small intestine. It secretes mucus and contains lymphatic tissue that makes antibodies. Antibodies are weapons of the immune system. They latch onto pathogens and tag them for destruction.

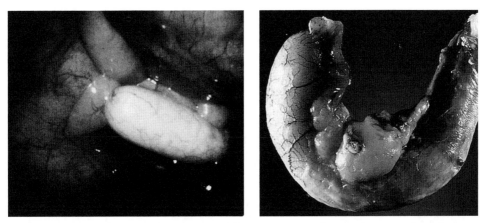

A healthy appendix, on the left, compared with an acute case of appendicitis, on the right, where the appendix is swollen and veins are dilated.

The opening from the appendix into the colon can be blocked. Mucus or feces can collect in it, or the swelling of lymph tissue can close it. Either way, bacteria that live inside are trapped there, and their numbers begin to grow. They invade the wall of the appendix or produce toxins that trigger inflammation. If the infection grows too great, the appendix can rupture, spreading infection throughout the abdomen.

The first sign of inflammation in the appendix is usually pain. It begins in a wide area around the navel, then moves to the lower right side of the abdomen. Loss of appetite, nausea, vomiting, and a fever can follow. Doctors say immediate removal of the appendix is the best way to avoid such serious complications. The immune system is not compromised because many other areas of lymphatic tissue also make antibodies.

People Say I'm So Skinny and Eat So Much That I Must Have a Tapeworm. They're Joking, Right?

Probably, but the truth is no laughing matter. Any suspected tapeworm infection demands immediate treatment. Tapeworms are parasites. They benefit from their happy home in the human gut, but the host suffers nausea, insatiable appetite, a swollen belly, weight loss, and abdominal pain. Advanced tapeworm infections can cause vitamin-deficiency diseases and intestinal blockage.

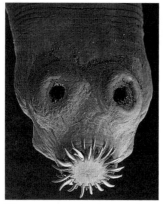

The tapeworm hooks onto its host with this spiked structure, the scolex. It has no mouth. It absorbs nutrients already digested by its hosts.

The tapeworm isn't the only uninvited guest in the human intestine. Others include roundworms, hookworms, whipworms, nematodes, and threadworms such as those shown here burrowing into the intestinal wall of a sheep.

Hookworm (left);
Nematodes (right)

Some tapeworms spend part of their life cycle in other animals. For example, the beef tapeworm, *Taenia saginata,* forms cysts in the muscle tissue of cattle. Humans get it from eating meat containing the cysts. Infection is rare in countries where meat is inspected. Other tapeworms form cysts in humans and develop as adults in other animals. Some of the more serious kinds include the hydatid tapeworm, *Echinococcus granulosis.* The adult worm lives in the intestines of dogs. Its eggs pass out in feces. Humans ingest the eggs when they get feces on their hands, either directly from contact with their pets or indirectly from the soil. Inside humans, cysts can form in the eyes, brain, and liver where they destroy tissue and disrupt functioning. The body's allergic reaction to a ruptured hydatid cyst can kill.

What Are the Nutritional Diseases? Nutritional diseases fall into four categories. The first is inadequate energy intake. Too little food means the body is starved for energy. The second type—too little protein—usually accompanies the first. It takes only a little meat, milk, fish, or plant protein to meet the body's protein needs, but many people lack even that.

Some 800 million people in today's world live in hunger.[2] Most of them live in India and Africa south of the Sahara. There, a diet of rice, yams, and green bananas may fill the belly, but it provides too few amino acids for humans—especially children—to grow, develop, and resist disease. Hunger is not entirely a third world problem. The USDA estimates that about 10 million U.S. families do not get enough food to meet their basic needs.[3]

The third type is a shortage of one or several vitamins or minerals. Such diseases result from a poor diet or from the body's failure to absorb the material. Two different forms of anemia are examples. The first, iron-deficiency anemia, can be treated with iron-rich foods and supplements. Pernicious anemia is different. It occurs when the body fails to absorb vitamin B_{12}, which is needed by the body for the process of iron absorption.

Diseases of the pancreas can produce vitamin deficiencies, too. Without pancreatic enzymes, fats do not break down in the small intestine. The fat-soluble vitamins A, D, E, and K are not absorbed. Vitamin deficiencies can also result from long-term vomiting or diarrhea. Inadequate diet during times of rapid growth—such as childhood, adolescence, or pregnancy—can also be at fault. See Table 3 on pages 150–151 for more information on deficiency diseases.

The fourth type of nutritional disease may surprise you. It is the disease of nutritional excess, or obesity. More than half of Americans are overweight, and nearly one in five is obese.[4] Obesity is a risk factor for such serious diseases as heart disease, diabetes, stroke, and more.

Can Too Much of a Vitamin or Mineral Cause Disease?

The body needs vitamins in only tiny amounts. Excesses of water-soluble vitamins are excreted in the urine. Fat-soluble vitamins are stored. They pose a risk to health if their levels rise too high. For example, too much vitamin D can cause muscle weakness, headaches, skin diseases, kidney damage, mental retardation, and life-threatening calcium deposits in blood vessels.

In some cases, we don't know how much is too much. Safe upper limits may be as great as 100 times the daily requirement—in the case of riboflavin—to as little as twice as much—in the case of zinc.[5] For other substances, such as niacin and potassium, more research is needed to find what the safe doses are.

What's
Heartburn, Who
Gets It, and How
Can It Be
Prevented or
Treated?

Heartburn is a bad name for a complaint that has nothing to do with the heart. Television ads call it acid indigestion. If it happens frequently, doctors call it GERD (for gastroesophageal reflux disease). It's a burning sensation that feels like it begins under the breastbone and moves up into the throat.

The pain may be at its worst when one is lying down or bending over. It may feel like bitter liquid rising into the throat or mouth.

It happens when acid escapes back through the valve at the top of the stomach and moves up the esophagus. Sixty million Americans say they get it at least once a month.[6] Heartburn is common after a big meal, and some foods—such as tomato sauce, fried food, sour beverages, coffee, or soft drinks—trigger it in some people. It's more common among people who are overweight, smoke, or drink too much alcohol. It can be associated with a stomach ulcer or a hiatal hernia, which is a bulge of part of the stomach into the chest cavity. The hernia causes the stomach valve to work improperly.

Some people find they can avoid heartburn by watching what they eat and drink, learning to relax, and not eating two or three hours before bedtime. Over-the-counter antacids are effective for many. For others, doctors recommend prescription drugs. In severe cases, a surgeon can stitch the valve tighter, preventing the backup of acid.

When the chemistry in the gallbladder isn't right, solid chunks form inside. They are usually made of cholesterol in combination with other substances—such as calcium—that crystallize. Most

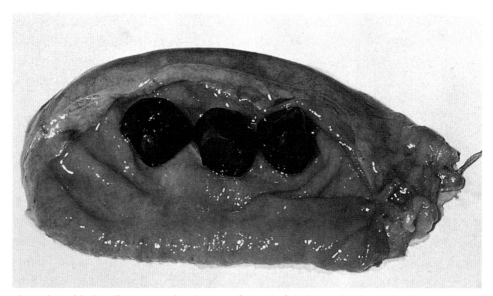

These three black gallstones are hard masses formed of cholesterol, bile, and calcium salts.

gallstones produce no symptoms and require no treatment. Those that do may cause a sharp pain in the upper right abdomen. That happens when stones lodge in the bile duct. Gallstones can be dangerous if they cause the gallbladder to enlarge and possibly rupture. In such cases, surgery is usually recommended.

In less severe cases, doctors treat the symptoms with antibiotics and painkillers. Drugs can dissolve the stones, or the gallbladder may be removed surgically. For some patients, crushing the stones is a good option. A crushing instrument can be passed through a fine tube into the gallbladder. An even newer technique uses shock waves applied to the outside of the body. In either case, the crushed gallstones pass out of the gallbladder in the bile.

What Is Celiac Disease, and How Is It Treated?

Also known as celiac sprue, this inherited disease is an intolerance to the protein gluten. Gluten is found in wheat, rye, barley, and (perhaps) oats. Although the symptoms are digestive, the cause actually lies in the intricate system of defenses against pathogens. In the person with celiac disease, the immune system gets it wrong. It reacts to the gluten in grains as if they were infectious agents. The attack of immune cells inflames the lining of the small intes-

Oakland Raiders' quarterback Rich Gannon with his daughter Danielle, who was born with celiac disease

tine. It may bring on diarrhea, weight loss, stomach cramps, pain in the joints, and skin rashes. The inflammation of the intestine impairs the body's ability to absorb nutrients from food. The result can be brittle bones (from too little calcium absorbed), colon cancer, poor growth, malnutrition, miscarriage, and birth defects.

Celiac disease is treated with a gluten-free diet. Avoiding gluten isn't easy. It's found not only in breads, pasta, and cereals but also in many processed foods—even soft drinks. Celiac disease runs in families, mostly those of northwestern European descent. Researchers at the Center for Celiac Research at the University of Maryland estimate that as many as one in every 150 Americans has it.[7]

What Is Diabetes?

There are two major kinds of diabetes. Their causes and treatments are different, but both involve insulin-glucose balance. Normally, eating signals the pancreas to increase insulin production. Insulin, once released into the blood, decreases the concentration of glucose molecules there. It sends glucose into cells, where it is used as an energy source.

Type 1, or insulin-dependent, diabetes is an autoimmune disease. It may be triggered by a viral infection. The immune system mistakes the insulin-producing cells of the pancreas for foreign invaders and destroys them. Very little or no insulin is produced. Without it, glucose remains in the blood. Body cells starve, deprived of their energy source. The body burns fat instead, causing weight loss and fatigue. Because the glucose level is too high in the blood, normal kidney action is disrupted. Glucose moves into the urine, taking water with it. That produces both frequent urination and extreme thirst. Type 1 diabetes typically runs in families. It usually begins in childhood or the teen years. The symptoms

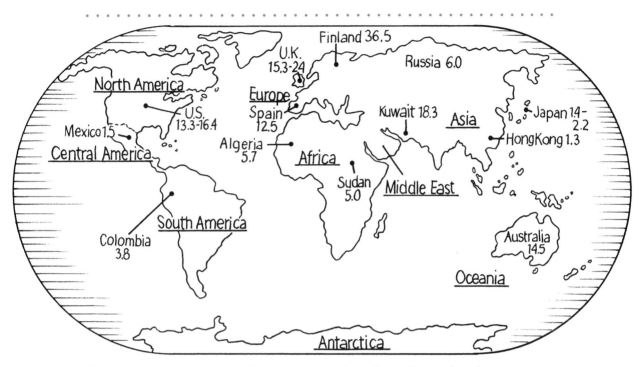

Type 1 diabetes is more common in some countries than others. The numbers shown are cases per 100,000 people age 14 and younger.

arise suddenly, usually within days. Type 1 is the rarer of the two major types. It accounts for only 5 to 10 percent of cases.

Far more common is Type 2, or insulin-resistant, diabetes. Of the nearly 16 million Americans who have diabetes, Type 2 accounts for 90–95 percent.[8] Type 2 tends to run in families, but it is not inherited in the same way as Type 1. The disease comes on gradually. It may begin with blurred vision, cuts and bruises that heal slowly, or numbness and tingling in feet or hands. Often, however, it starts with no obvious symptoms and goes unrecognized in perhaps a third of cases.[9]

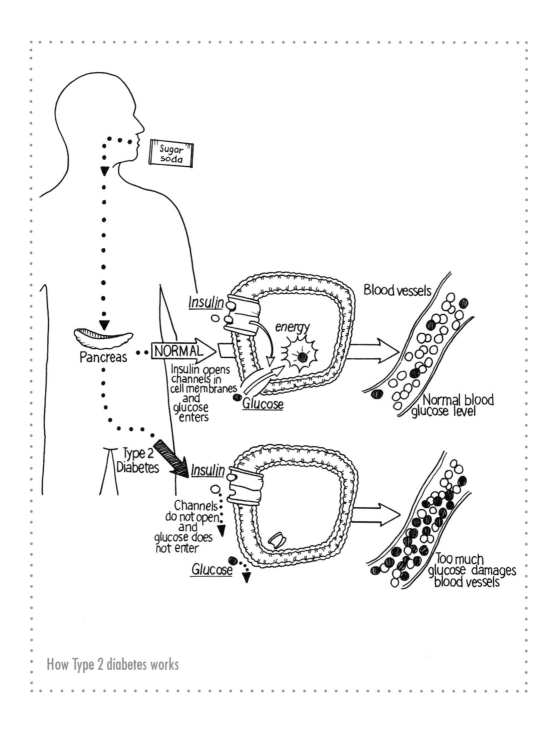

Sugar soda

Insulin

energy

Blood vessels

Pancreas

NORMAL

Insulin opens channels in cell membranes and glucose enters

Glucose

Normal blood glucose level

Type 2 Diabetes

Insulin

Channels do not open and glucose does not enter

Glucose

Too much glucose damages blood vessels

How Type 2 diabetes works

Type 2 diabetes occurs when the pancreas makes enough insulin, but body cells resist its action. Cells starve for glucose, not because insulin is lacking, but because they fail to respond to its command. The pancreas spews out more and more insulin, but cells become increasingly resistant. Eventually, insulin-making cells stop working. In the meantime, high concentrations of glucose and insulin in the blood take a toll. Glucose weakens capillary walls and blocks small arteries. Bleeding in tiny capillaries injures the retina in the eye. Poor circulation causes ulcers on the legs and feet. The liver increases its output of the "bad cholesterol" carriers, LDLs. That may increase the risk of heart disease by as much as 20 percent.[10]

Once a disease of middle to later life, Type 2 is growing more common among young people. Some 20 to 30 percent of diabetic children and teens now have Type 2, compared with one-tenth that number a generation ago.[11] About 800,000 new cases of Type 2 diabetes are diagnosed in the United States each year. That's about one every 30 seconds.[12]

"Diabetes is already the number-one cause of blindness, amputations, and kidney failure, and it increases by two or three times the risk of heart attack or stroke," says Robert Sherwin, president of the American Diabetes Association.[13] Sherwin worries about rising numbers of diabetes cases—up nearly a third from 4.9 to 6.5 percent between 1990 and 1998. The increase in the number of children and teens with diabetes is "extraordinarily worrying," says Arthur Rubinstein, dean of the Mount Sinai School of Medicine in New York. "If people become diabetic at age 10 or 15 or 20, you can predict that when they are 30 or 40, they could have terrible complications.[14]

How Is Diabetes Treated? People with Type 1 diabetes take insulin injections daily and monitor their blood glucose levels closely. Weight control, exercise, and healthy foods are the cornerstones of treatment for Type 2. Weight loss decreases insulin production. Regular exercise speeds the use of sugar in cells. The fiber in vegetables, fruits, beans, and whole grains slows the absorption of sugars into the blood from the intestine. Drugs may be prescribed to:

- increase body cell sensitivity to insulin, especially in the muscles;

- slow the absorption of carbohydrates into the blood from the intestine;

- stimulate pancreatic cells to make more insulin;

- retard the conversion of glycogen to glucose in the liver.

Can Diabetes Be Prevented? As far as we know, nothing prevents Type 1, but "at least 75 percent of new cases of Type 2 diabetes can be prevented," says Jo Ann Manson, an endocrine specialist at Harvard Medical School.[15] How? "Type 2 diabetes . . . is epidemic in industrialized societies and is strongly associated with obesity," says Claire Steppan, an endocrinologist at the University of Pennsylvania.[16] The association is significant. One study showed that overweight women faced a five times greater risk of diabetes than their healthy-weight peers. Obese women faced a risk 28 to 93 times greater![17]

Steppan found that fat cells secrete a signaling molecule she calls resistin. The more fat cells, the more resistin. The more resistin, the more insulin-resistant muscle cells become. According to Steppan, resistin is the hormone that links obesity to diabetes. Since four out of five people who develop Type 2 diabetes are overweight, the conclusion is apparent.[18] Too many fat cells make too much resistin.

Researchers at Boston's Beth Israel Deaconess Medical Center agree. They have found a substance released by fat cells that travels through the blood and impairs insulin action in muscle and liver cells. Fat, they say, acts as an endocrine organ. It makes substances that affect other organs. "Adipose [fat] tissue is more than capable of telling other energy-storing organs what to do," says University of Pennsylvania physician Morris Birnbaum.[19]

The prescription for prevention, then, is to maintain a healthy weight. Keeping the number and size of fat cells optimal helps to keep insulin and sugar in balance. The only way to maintain a healthy weight is to control portion sizes, go easy on the goodies, and ask for seconds on exercise. Even for people who aren't overweight, healthy foods play a role in prevention. In one study, men who consumed more than 8.1 grams of cereal fiber daily (about the same as a cup of raisin bran) cut their risk of Type 2 diabetes by 30 percent, compared with men who ate less than 3.2 grams per day.[20]

Exercise is important too. A brisk walk daily lowers blood sugar, increases insulin sensitivity, and decreases body fat. "Exercise is probably the best medication on the market to treat insulin resistance," says Canadian physician Jean-Pierre Despres.[21] "The risk of Type 2 diabetes is reduced by 25 percent among people who are moderately vigorously active," says Ralph Paffenbarger, an epidemiologist at Stanford University.[22]

Can a Pancreas Transplant Cure People With Type 1 Diabetes?

Yes, and some 14,000 patients have had them.[23] The transplanted pancreas can be a partial organ from a living donor or an entire organ from a deceased donor. The operation frees the transplant recipient from dependence on insulin. It also can prevent the serious side effects of diabetes such as heart disease, kidney disease, and blindness.

A pancreas transplant isn't for everyone, however. It requires a lifetime of taking immune-suppressing drugs to block organ rejection. Such drugs compromise the body's ability to fight off infections and certain cancers.

In the future, whole-organ transplants may not be necessary. Since the 1980s, doctors have been experimenting with transplanting only the insulin-producing beta cells of the pancreas. One approach tested at the Diabetes Research Institute in Miami combines stem cells from bone-marrow cells with pancreatic cells. (Stem cells are unspecialized. They can develop into many different kinds of cells.) The stem cells, which play a role in determining what the immune system will ignore or attack, might block rejection of transplanted cells.[24]

A different approach looks promising to researchers at the University of Alberta. They have altered the genes in K cells of the duodenum of mice. The engineered K cells have been made to work much as normal beta cells do. They can make insulin and store it for release later, when blood sugar levels rise. In trials, the K cells have produced enough insulin to prevent Type 1 diabetes in animals.[25]

My Aunt Was Diabetic When She Was Pregnant. Now She's Not. How Can That Be?

Your aunt probably developed gestational diabetes. (Gestation is the time period when the infant is developing inside its mother's body.) Two to 5 percent of pregnant women do. It happens because hormones produced by the placenta—the organ that nourishes

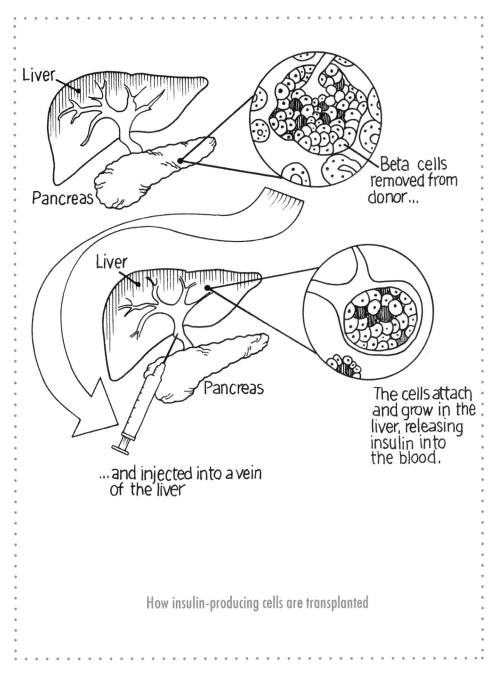

Liver

Pancreas

Beta cells
removed from
donor...

Liver

Pancreas

...and injected into a vein
of the liver

The cells attach
and grow in the
liver, releasing
insulin into
the blood.

How insulin-producing cells are transplanted

the fetus—interfere with the mother's insulin-glucose control system. Gestational diabetes can often be controlled with diet, although some women need drugs.

Treatment is important because gestational diabetes increases risks of overly large babies. Large infants face higher risks for difficult deliveries and birth by cesarean section. They also face a greater risk of diabetes in adult life than normal-weight infants.

Gestational diabetes usually disappears when pregnancy ends, but your aunt should have blood-sugar checks regularly. Gestational diabetes increases the risk of Type 2 developing later in life.

My Doctor Says I Have Irritable Bowel Syndrome. What Is It, and What Can I Do About It?

Irritable bowel syndrome (IBS) is also called irritable or spastic colon. It causes pain after eating, which goes away after a bowel movement. The pain results from strong, rapid contractions of the intestine. Other symptoms of IBS include cramps, bloating, constipation, and diarrhea. Twenty percent of Americans have it—two-thirds of them female and most of them undiagnosed.[26] IBS usually starts in the teens or twenties. It's often associated with stress.

Doctors tell their patients to keep a food diary to find out what triggers their symptoms. Large meals, cold or carbonated drinks, or the lactose in dairy products (see next question) are sometimes at fault. It may stem from eating or drinking too rapidly, chewing gum, smoking, or nervously swallowing air. Coffee and caffeinated soft drinks, vitamin C supplements, and artificial sweeteners are sometimes the villains. Eating fiber-rich foods and exercising regularly help regulate bowel action. Doctors prescribe drugs to slow the movement of food through the colon and to relieve painful spasms.

New research suggests that microbes in the intestine may cause IBS, at least in some people. In 2000, doctors at California's Cedars–Sinai Medical Center tested IBS patients for small intestinal bacterial overgrowth, SIBO. Finding too many bacteria present in nearly 80 percent, they prescribed antibiotics. "On the whole, we found a significant reduction in the symptoms of IBS," says researcher Mark Pimentel.[27]

Why Can't Some People Drink Milk and Eat Ice Cream?

Lactose is the sugar found naturally in milk and other dairy products. Break that molecule apart and two molecules are formed: one of glucose and the other of galactose. In childhood, nearly two out of every three adults in the world stop making the enzyme that splits galactose.[28] (Caucasians of European ancestry are an exception.) Lactose-intolerant individuals can often eat cheese or yogurt because the bacteria used in making those foods break down galactose. Lactose-free products and tablets that contain lactose-digesting enzymes can lessen or prevent symptoms.

Is Inflammatory Bowel Disease (IBD) the Same as Irritable Bowel Syndrome (IBS)?

No, although the symptoms of both include diarrhea, abdominal cramps, fever, and loss of both weight and appetite.

Inflammatory bowel disease is—as its name suggests—inflammation. Colon tissue becomes irritated, swollen, and painful—just as a cut finger does when the immune system mounts an attack on microbes that might invade the wound. Two kinds of IBD are Crohn's disease and ulcerative colitis. Doctors often treat IBD with a drug that counteracts TNF-α (tumor necrosis factor alpha), a product of the immune system that produces inflammation. In severe cases, physicians may prescribe drugs that suppress a broader range of immune-system products and functions. Surgeons may remove seriously inflamed tissue.

What Kinds of Cancers Develop in the Digestive System?

Cancer is uncontrolled cell growth. Cells that shouldn't divide do, forming a mass of cells, or tumor. Cells malfunction because of a change in the master control molecule in their nuclei. That molecule is DNA. Radiation, chemicals, and aging can damage it; or changes can happen purely by chance. Cancer cells can spread from one organ to another through the blood or lymphatic system. (Lymph is clear fluid that bathes cells. It does not circulate in the blood vessels, but rather through its own system of glands, ducts, and nodes.)

Cancer can occur in any part of the body, including the organs of the digestive system:

- **Mouth and throat:** Warning signs include sores that do not heal, a lump in the mouth or gums, bleeding, a persistent sore throat, pain, or swelling. Smoking and drinking too much alcohol increase the risk for cancers of the mouth and throat. Exposure to the sun accounts for the majority of tumors on the lips. Half of all cancers in the cheek are associated with the use of smokeless tobacco. Together, cancers in the mouth and throat account for nearly 3 percent of all cancers and 2 percent of cancer deaths in the United States.[29]

- **Esophagus:** Cancer of the esophagus is one of the most aggressive and deadly forms. More than 70 percent of patients die within three years after diagnosis. It can strike anyone, but is more likely in those who smoke or drink too much alcohol. Reflux disease, the backup of stomach acid into the esophagus, also increases risks.

- **Stomach:** Cancer of the stomach was common in the United States until the 1940s. Its death rate has dropped by two-thirds since then, perhaps because we eat less smoked and cured meat. Nevertheless, about 24,000 people per year learn that they have gastric (stomach) cancer. It is hard to diagnose early. Its symptoms may include indigestion, nausea, fatigue, diarrhea or constipation, and loss of appetite.

- **Liver:** The normal, healthy liver performs more functions than any other organ—except, perhaps, the brain. It stores vitamins and minerals, reconstructs molecules from food into a form the body can use, and moderates the levels of glucose in the blood by storing or converting glycogen as needed. It helps maintain the proper balance of fluid in blood and cells, makes proteins that clot blood, and detoxifies drugs and chemicals. Tumors that form in the liver interfere with one or more of these functions. Cancers of the liver cells, or hepatocytes, account for more than 8 out of 10 liver cancers.[30] Having the liver disease hepatitis increases the risk of liver cancer. So do alcohol and tobacco use, poisons such as arsenic in the water supply, and steroid drugs. Liver cancer is seldom diagnosed early because its symptoms are subtle or absent.

- **Pancreas:** Cancer of the pancreas accounts for about 5 percent of all cancer deaths in the United States. It is the fourth-leading cause

of cancer death. Pancreatic cancers are particularly aggressive. The survival rate after two years is only 10 percent.[31] Most pancreatic cancers form in the lining of the duct that connects the pancreas and the small intestine. Although pancreatic cancer is two to three times more common among smokers than nonsmokers, the exact cause is not known. Pancreatic tumors are silent killers. They produce few if any symptoms before they have spread to the liver or lungs. Diabetes increases the risk of pancreatic cancer, as does a diet high in meat and fat and low in fruits and vegetables.

- **Colon:** Cancer of the small intestine is rare, but cancers of the large intestine and rectum kill nearly 60,000 Americans a year. It

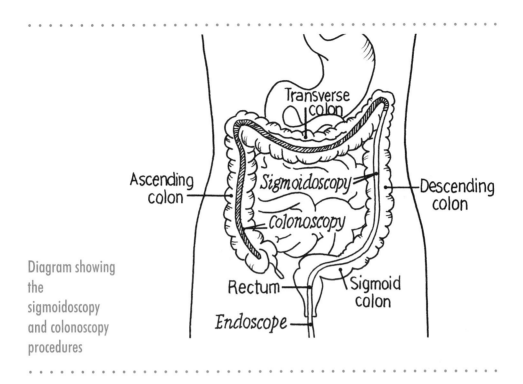

Diagram showing the sigmoidoscopy and colonoscopy procedures

can arise from inflammatory bowel disease, although many cases have no known cause. Other risk factors include a high-fat diet, obesity, and lack of exercise. Some forms of colon cancer are hereditary, but many cases may be preventable. The vitamin folate seems to thwart its development. Despite the protection offered by five servings of folate-rich fruits and vegetables daily, only 20 percent of Americans get enough.[32] Some cancers are easier to detect and treat than others. Pancreatic and liver cancer can progress without symptoms or warning signs. So can colon cancer, but it's highly curable if detected early. It may be found from tests for blood in the feces or by using any of several colon-cancer screening tests. One such test is sigmoidoscopy, performed with a tiny tube containing a fiber-optic viewing device. It can discover precancerous polyps in the lower third of the colon.

The more accurate procedure is colonoscopy, an examination of the entire length of the large intestine—about 150 centimeters, or 5 feet.[33] The American Cancer Society recommends that all people have a colonoscopy at age 50 and every five years after that.

The wave of the future may be "virtual colonoscopy." It delivers a three-dimensional picture using a CT scanner. (CT stands for computerized tomography, a computer-assisted X-ray technique.) Another developing technique is testing the DNA from colorectal tumor cells eliminated in feces.

Like other cancers, tumors of the digestive system may be treated with one or more of the following methods:

- **Chemotherapy,** or the use of drugs that kill cancer cells. Most anticancer drugs are given by injection. A few are taken by mouth. Usually, the drugs enter the blood and circulate throughout the body. Sometimes, the drugs may be injected directly into the organ affected, as in the case of stomach cancer.

- **Radiation,** or the use of high-energy rays and particles to kill tumor cells or slow their growth. It is often effective against small tumors. Some radiation is delivered from machines that focus a beam of radiation. For some cancers, rods or pellets of radioactive material may be implanted in or near the tumor. Implants deliver a continuous dose of radiation over time.

- **Surgery,** or the removal of a tumor, all or in part. Surgical removal of precancerous polyps in the colon can be 100 percent effective in fighting colon cancer. Surgery to remove a tumor after cancer cells have spread to other organs is not effective.

- **Immunotherapy,** or biological therapy, the use of the body's own immune defenses to destroy tumor cells. Substances that mimic or enhance the body's natural immune responses to invaders are injected into the bloodstream.

What Is Anorexia Nervosa, and How Is It Treated?

Shakespeare called appetite "a universal wolf." For the person with anorexia nervosa, the wolf ravages inside, silent and deadly. The term anorexia means "loss of appetite." That's not a good name for the disease, because people who have it do not lose their desire to eat. Rather, they keep their appetite under rigid control and do not eat enough food. They are constantly at war with their bodies.

In people who do not have anorexia, a hormone produced in the digestive track, cholecystokinin (CCK), signals the brain when the stomach is full. The CCK system malfunctions in those with anorexia. They feel full after only a few bites. People with anorexia are terrified of gaining weight. They have unreal images of their bodies, seeing fat where there is none. The effects of anorexia, just like other forms of starvation, include:

- Frequent, sometimes fatal, diarrhea

- Shrinkage of the heart muscle

- Reduced volume of blood pumped

- Slow heart rate

- Low blood pressure

- Slow breathing rate

- Reduced lung capacity

- Respiratory failure

- Smaller ovaries in women; smaller testes in men

- Loss of interest in sex

- Cessation of menstrual periods in women

- Reduced muscle size and strength

- Reduced capacity for work and exercise

- Anemia

- Fluid accumulation in the skin

- The growth of a fine coating of hair, called lanugo

- Impaired ability to fight infections and repair wounds

- Potassium deficiency leading to heart disorders

- Calcium loss from the bones leading to osteoporosis

- Low body temperature (hypothermia)—frequently a major contributor to death

- Heart failure and death

Anorexia usually begins with an attempt to shed a few pounds. Then weight loss becomes an obsession. Constantly fighting food and exercising to the point of exhaustion makes the anorectic feel in control of life. In a society that worships thinness, the anorectic strives for an impossible ideal. Katherine Halmi and her colleagues at New York Presbyterian Hospital studied concern over mistakes, personal standards, doubts, and expectations among more than 300 anorexic women. They found evidence of an extreme strive for perfectionism. The more severe the disorder, the greater the perfectionist drive,[34] and the more serious the consequences.

Inheritance plays a role in anorexia. Genes make some individuals more vulnerable than others. Identical twins are eight times more likely to both develop anorexia than are fraternal twins.[35] Nevertheless, anorexia develops only in certain cultures. Anorexia is most common in the United States and some other industrialized nations. The Western influence is, unfortunately, spreading. "In Hong Kong, mainland China, and Taiwan, places influenced more and more by the weight-consciousness of the West, the number of people with eating disorders is growing rapidly," says Dr. George Hsu of Boston's New England Medical Center.[36]

As many as 5 in every 100 young females have anorexia. Boys and men become anorexic, too, but in fewer numbers—less than 1 in every 100.[37] Males are less likely than females to starve themselves. They opt instead for grueling regimens of exercise. The disease is treated with intravenous feeding, supervised eating, counseling, and therapy. Doctors often prescribe supplements of vitamin D and calcium. Those nutrients reduce the risk of osteoporosis that accompanies anorexia. Some 10 percent of teenagers with anorexia die from the disease.[38]

What Is Bulimia, and How Is It Treated?

People with bulimia consume large quantities of food quickly. Then they vomit or take enemas or laxatives to expel the food. Frequent vomiting causes sores and rupturing in the esophagus. Stomach acid erodes teeth. Salivary glands swell. Broken blood vessels make the eyes look bloodshot. Fluids collect under the skin, causing a chubby-cheeked look. Imbalances in blood chemistry can trigger heart failure. Bulimia affects as many as 3 in every 100 females and about 2 in every 1,000 males.[39]

Bulimia and anorexia are alike in some ways. Both develop in people-pleasers who have a hard time expressing their feelings. Both anorexics and bulimics develop folic acid, zinc, and vitamin B_6 deficiencies. Both have been linked with low levels of the neurotransmitter serotonin in the brain. The same shortage happens with depression, and anorexics and bulimics are often depressed. (For reasons no one understands, serotonin-enhancing drugs help many who are depressed or bulimic, but they do not help anorectics.)

People with bulimia are more aware of their problem than are anorectics. While anorectics grow increasingly thin, bulimics usually maintain a normal weight. Their disorder, however, saps them of strength and energy. While female anorectics may cease having periods altogether, bulimics usually have them, but irregularly. The most serious dangers of bulimia lie in dehydration (loss of too much water) and damage to the bowels, liver, and kidneys. An imbalance of salts in the blood can lead to irregular heart action and heart failure.

With both anorexia and bulimia, the most frequent triggering event is dieting. With magazines and books full of diets and store shelves groaning under the weight of diet products, dieting is hard to avoid. But experts advise: "Don't do it!" Eat sensibly when you are hungry. If you need to lose a few pounds, ask for help from a registered dietitian or your doctor. Enjoy your body, your food, and your life.

The Mad Cow Menace

When Stanley Prusiner first suggested that proteins could cause disease, few scientists took him seriously. They thought all diseases were caused by living things that contain genetic material. DNA and RNA take control of the cell when a virus or bacterium infects it. Proteins are merely products of genetic control. How could they cause disease?

Despite the skeptics, Prusiner continued his experiments with proteins he called prions (pronounced PREE-ons, for proteinaceous infectious particles). He took brain material from sheep infected with a disease called scrapie. He injected it into healthy animals. They got the disease. When he irradiated the brain tissue with ultraviolet light—a measure that destroys genetic material—it still caused the disease.

In sheep, the prion in normal brain cells has a spiral backbone. The scrapie type forms a flat sheet. Prusiner thought the scrapie prion caused normal prions to change shape. An experiment proved him right. He mixed the two forms in a test tube. The normal form changed shape when mixed with the scrapie form. No one knows exactly what the normal prion does in cells, but it seems to have something to do with binding copper.[40]

In 1986 the first case of "mad cow" disease, or bovine spongiform encephalopathy (BSE), was found in cattle in Great Britain. Irritable personalities, fearful behavior, and a staggering gait preceded death in affected cows. Autopsies showed holes in their brain tissue. Food scientists thought the cows got BSE from their feed. The feed contained meat and bonemeal from sheep that had died of scrapie.

Scrapie and BSE are both prion diseases. They take a long time to produce symptoms. Years pass while normal prions change shape. Still more years go by before the misshapen prions accumulate in numbers large enough to cause brain damage. Exactly how the damage occurs is unknown. In cell cultures, the shape change happens inside nerve cells, where misshapen prions accumulate in pockets called lysosomes. The bursting of lysosomes could kill brain cells. The natural cleanup of dead cells by the body could leave the spongy spaces in the brain characteristic of the prion diseases.

A human disease similar to BSE is Creutzfeldt-Jakob Disease (CJD). CJD begins with numbness and unex-plained mood swings. Next come hallucinations, staggering, and pain. Before death in one or two years, people with CJD lose sight, memory, personality, and physical control. There is no treatment or cure.

Autopsies show spongy tissue in the brain of CJD victims. The pockets look similar to those found in the brains of BSE-infected cattle and scrapie-infected sheep. But the diseases were different, scientists and government officials insisted. They believed in the protection of the "species barrier"—that a disease that infects one kind of animal won't infect another. People don't get scrapie from eating infected lamb or mutton, they said. Humans shouldn't get CJD from eating beef infected with BSE either—or so the thinking went.

Despite their faith in the species barrier, the British government took steps to curb the spread of BSE. In 1988 it banned animal feed made from the brains and spinal cords of cattle and sheep. Slaughterhouses often ignored the ban, which was poorly enforced. Nervous-system remains from cows that might have been infected continued to be processed into human and animal food. The number of BSE cows continued to rise, reaching a peak of 36,680 in 1992.[41]

As BSE numbers grew, more people worried that eating meat from BSE cows might cause CJD in people. Scientists and government leaders assured the public that it could not. Early in the 1990s, a disease resembling BSE was found among cats. This warning sign that prion diseases could cross the species barrier was ignored.

Before the 1990s, CJD was extremely rare. Worldwide, it occurred only once in every million people, nearly always between the ages of 50 and 75.[42] The incidence of CJD among humans in Britain nearly doubled between 1990 and 1994.[43] By 1996, laboratory investigations had revealed a tragedy. A new strain of CJD called variant CJD (vCJD) had turned up in British people.

Variant CJD arises much earlier in life than the previously known CJD. Misshapen prions in beef cause it. BSE spread because brains and spinal cords of dead cows were fed to other cattle. Transmission to humans occurred through brain and organ meats and "mechanically recovered beef" scraped from the spines of cattle.[44] The species barrier had been breached—not by a virus or bacterium—but by a protein. On March 20, 1996, the British government admitted that vCJD had been found in ten people under the age of 42, half of them associated with the meat or livestock industry. Some of the people were teenagers.[45]

"BSE spread like a chain letter," while the public was "sedated by the official presentation of risk," noted an official investigator.[46] By the year 2000, nearly 200,000 British cattle were known to be infected with BSE. More than 4 million cows had been slaughtered, and 81 people had died from vCJD.[47] The British beef industry lay in ruins.

Because the disease might take fifteen years or more to produce symptoms in people, experts predict a rising human death rate from vCJD in the twenty-first century. For fear of spreading the disease, people who spent more than six months in the United Kingdom between 1980 and 1996 are not allowed to donate blood in the United States.

If some are born to greatness, others must wait their turn. Stanley Prusiner—who suggested the prion basis for disease in 1980—didn't get his Nobel Prize until 1997.

· · · ·

CHAPTER FOUR

19

QUESTIONS
**ABOUT
FOOD SAFETY**

*Consumers go to the supermarket thinking everything [there] is
clean, and that is just not true. People can't assume that anymore.
Consumers have a responsibility in food safety.*

• DONALD H. BURR •

RESEARCH MICROBIOLOGIST WITH THE U.S. FOOD AND DRUG ADMINISTRATION

**Does
Government
Regulation
Guarantee
That All Food
Is Safe?**

Food products approved by the U.S. Food and Drug Administration (FDA) are carefully tested. "Approval means that our scientists have concluded that there's a reasonable certainty that no harm will result from the intended use of the food ingredient," says George Pauli of that agency.[1] The law does not, however, require that all foods be tested or all health claims be evaluated. For example, herbal preparations sold as dietary supplements or as medicines are exempt from FDA testing.

> **This Product Contains Olestra.** Olestra may cause abdominal cramping and loose stools. Olestra inhibits the absorption of some vitamins and other nutrients. Vitamins A, D, E, and K have been added.

The warning label found on products containing Olestra

Are Artificial Sweeteners and Fat Substitutes Safe?

The next time you shop at a supermarket, read the labels on products specifically marketed for diabetics and people who are trying to lose weight. Many contain substitutes for sugar and fat that provide taste with fewer calories. One example is the artificial sweetener aspartame. It is made from two amino acids. The body digests it and uses it as protein. Because tiny amounts produce an intense sweet flavor, it's nearly calorie-free. Another no-calorie sweetener is sucralose. It is made from table sugar, but chlorine atoms bind certain sites on the molecule, making it indigestible.

A popular fat substitute is olestra. It is a sugar molecule combined with eight fatty-acid molecules. (Digestible fats are a glycerol with three fatty acids attached.) The shape of the molecule prevents digestive enzymes from attacking it. It tastes like fat but adds no calories to food.

Artificial "foods" such as these must pass many tests before the FDA approves them. However, research cannot prove them totally risk-free, and most have their advocates and their critics. Saccharin is a good example. It's been available since 1879, but controversy arose as early as 1911. That year, a board of scientists recommended that it be banned, but popular demand kept it on the market. Over time, saccharin earned a position on the FDA's "GRAS" list. GRAS means "Generally Recognized as Safe."

Fears resurfaced in the 1970s. Rats given high doses of saccharin developed bladder cancer. Scientists again proposed a ban, but consumers and food manufacturers objected. Saccharin was the only artificial sweetener available then. In 1977 the FDA struck a compromise. Saccharin remained on supermarket shelves but bore a warning label.

In 2000 the National Toxicology Program removed saccharin from its list of cancer-causing chemicals. The FDA's warning label was discontinued later that year.

"We welcome the news that saccharin-sweetened products will no longer carry an outdated and misleading warning label," said a representative of the food industry.[2] Not everyone agreed. "The government is making a serious mistake in delisting saccharin (from its list of carcinogens)," said Michael Jacobson of the Center for Science in the Public Interest.[3]

Olestra seems ready to accumulate a similar, controversial history. In 1996, the FDA approved its use in snack foods, but all olestra-containing products had to bear a warning label. The label said that olestra could cause cramps and diarrhea in some people. It warned that the fat substitute might interfere with the absorption of vitamins A, D, E, and K. The label caused a lot of confusion. Some people thought that olestra would make them sick for sure. Others thought that olestra-containing foods were good sources of the vitamins mentioned on the label.

Further research showed that olestra lowered the levels of carotenoids in the blood. (Carotenoids are substances in food that the body converts to vitamin A.) Such a loss might increase the risk of cancer, although raising carotenoid levels has not been shown to reduce that risk. While the food industry continues to promote olestra, critics counter with many doubts and cautions. Says the Center for Science in the Public Interest: "Any benefits of olestra do not outweigh the risks." Consumers may not agree. In olestra's first two years, 80 million bags of olestra chips were sold.[4]

Three major causes are:

1. **Enzyme action.** The same enzymes that ripen fruit also spoil it. Protein-splitting enzymes in meat break down its structure.

2. **Oxidation.** When oxygen from the air reacts with fats, larger fatty acids break into smaller ones. The by-products smell bad, and fatty foods such as butter turn rancid. Oxidation also turns sliced apples and bananas brown.

3. **Microbial action.** Bacteria, fungi, and yeast digest food, using the energy they obtain from it to live and reproduce. Spoilage is the first phase of decay. Leave foods out long enough, and microorganisms recycle all the atoms in them.

Some spoilage announces its presence. Food looks unappetizing, feels slimy, or smells foul. You don't need to be warned to avoid it. Some spoilage gives no such warning, and that's where the danger lies. Perhaps the best-known example is botulism. When the bacterium *Clostridium botulinum* grows in foods, it releases a toxin. The toxin is destroyed by heat, but it survives careless canning or cooking. Once inside the body, the toxin attacks the nervous system. It causes nausea, weakness, and muscular paralysis. Paralysis of respiratory muscles is the most serious complication and, generally, the cause of death. Before 1950, botulism killed 60 percent of the people who got it. Today, medical procedures that assist breathing until the toxin breaks down have cut the death rate to 5 percent.[5]

It can't entirely. All food will spoil eventually, but spoiling can be slowed. The rate depends on temperature, the kind of food, the kind and number of organisms present, moisture, and time. Most spoilage organisms grow best between 70° and 100° Fahrenheit (21° and 38° Celsius). At temperatures below 40° F (4° C), enzyme action and microbial growth slow. They don't stop completely, however. Some food additives can slow spoilage, too.

Drying is another way to slow spoilage. When microorganisms digest food, enzymes move out through their cell walls into the food. The enzymes break down the food's molecular structure. Molecules then move back through the cell wall into the microorganism. They move either by passive diffusion or by active transport, in which the cell uses energy to move molecules. The enzymes must be in water for these processes to occur. That's why moist foods spoil more rapidly than dry ones. It's also the reason why drying retards spoilage. The organisms are there, but without water they cannot feed.

Cooking foods to an internal temperature of 160° F (71° C) kills many kinds of disease-causing organisms. (Microwaved foods need extra protection against spoilage before cooking because they may not get hot enough in the oven.) Pasteurization slows the spoilage of milk. It requires a temperature of 145° F (63° C) maintained for 30 minutes. Outbreaks of disease have occurred when careless processors or faulty equipment have delivered lower temperatures for shorter periods.

Cooking and pasteurization stop spoilage for a while. It starts again when organisms from the environment get into the food. They come from air, human contact, machines, wrapping materials, dust, insects, and other sources. Washing fruits and vegetables removes some—but not all—spoilage organisms. Covering and wrapping food provide a barrier against contamination.

The numbers of microorganisms in the food make a big difference. For example, if a bacterial population doubles every 20 minutes (which many do at room temperature), an initial contamination of two microorganisms would reach a population size of a little more than 1,000 in three hours. That sounds like a lot, but in microbial terms it's a small number and may not do much damage. If, however, the initial number was 1,000, bacterial numbers can swell to more than a half million in the same length of time. That's enough to spoil food and (perhaps) cause illness in the unlucky diner.

What Causes Food Poisoning?

Bacteria, viruses, fungi, and microscopic animals need food, and they often use the same sources you do. In the process, their numbers grow. Once inside the human body they may invade and kill cells of the intestinal tract. Some travel through the blood and attack other organs. Some release waste products that can prove hazardous, even fatal, to humans.

Microbes that cause disease—either directly through their life activities or indirectly through their toxins—are called pathogens. Some 200 different kinds produce 76 million cases of food poisoning and cause 5,000 deaths annually in the United States.[6] Symptoms typically include nausea, vomiting, and diarrhea. Among the perpetrators of all this mayhem are:

- *Salmonella*, a rod-shaped bacterium. It penetrates the lining of the small intestine. The lining gets inflamed when the immune system fights back. *Salmonella*'s favorite haunt is the backyard barbecue. Cut up chicken on a board or plate, grill it, and then put it back on the same surface, and surprise! The cooked chicken has been "reinfected" with the "bugs" from the uncooked one. *Salmonella* is also a frequent resident of raw eggs and milk. It triggers severe diarrhea or worse, infecting from two to four million Americans annually.[7]

- *Listeria,* a bacterium that swims with a long, whiplike tail. It is another gate-crasher at barbecues. Undercooked chicken and hot dogs are the source in about 20 percent of cases.[8] *Listeria* doesn't mind cold temperatures. It grows in refrigerated foods, such as cheese, ice cream, and milk. It causes nausea, stomach cramps, and fever as it invades the cells of the intestinal lining. If it spreads through the blood to other organs, it can have more serious consequences, including miscarriage and stillbirth among pregnant women.

- *Shigella,* another rod-shaped bacterium, accounts for about 10 percent of the foodborne illnesses in the United States.[9] It's yet another uninvited guest at picnics and barbecues, lurking in chicken and salads. It invades and destroys cells in the intestinal lining. Some strains produce a powerful poison.

- *Campylobacter,* a thin, rod-shaped bacterium that swims. It's the leading cause of bacterial diarrhea, infecting up to four million Americans a year.[10] Researchers aren't sure how it does its dirty work. It may produce a poison, or it may invade intestinal cells. Surveys show that 20 to 100 percent of supermarket chickens carry it, as can water and milk.[11]

- *Vibrio,* a curved, rod-shaped bacterium that lives in the ocean. It's a common source of bacterial infection from raw or undercooked shellfish. More than 8,000 illnesses and 57 deaths occur annually in the United States from *Vibrio* infections.[12] The life-threatening disease cholera, which kills millions in the developing world every year, is caused by a species of *Vibrio.*

- *Viruses,* such as the Norwalk virus, named for an unlucky town in Ohio where it was first identified in 1972. The Norwalk virus and its relatives have single strains of RNA (not DNA) as their genetic material. They hang around city water supplies, wells, swimming pools, shellfish markets, and salad bars. The Norwalk virus and its relatives are responsible for 23,000,000 illnesses among Americans each year.[13]

- *Cryptosporidium*, not a virus or a bacterium, but a single-celled animal. It's a parasite, living inside the cells of humans, cattle, and other animals. It infects the small intestine and releases its eggs into feces. It enters new hosts when food or water becomes contaminated with sewage or runoff from farms. Outbreaks among people have been traced to drinking water, apple cider, and homemade chicken salad. Some people get it from kittens or puppies. It's common. Somewhere between 30 and 50 percent of the U.S. population has developed immunity against it.[14]

- "*Unknown agents.*" This is the most important category of all. More than 80 percent of foodborne illness has an unidentified cause.[15]

What Are These E. Coli Outbreaks I Hear About So Often?

Were the German bacteriologist Theodor Escherich alive today, he might refuse the honor of having the organism he discovered named after him. In 1885 he isolated some rod-shaped bacteria from the human colon. Most strains of his namesake, *Escherichia coli*—or *E. coli* for short—are harmless. Their presence in water or food, however, indicates contact with human sewage or animal wastes.

The strain that has caused most trouble recently is *E. coli* O157:H7. It thrives in ground meat, unpasteurized juices, alfalfa sprouts, lettuce, and other produce. O157 made headlines in 1982 when it infected 42 customers of a fast-food chain in two states. In 1996, 70 people in the western United States and Canada got the infection from unpasteurized apple cider.[16] In 2000, 60 people in Wisconsin got *E. coli* at a steak house, and a three-year-old child died.[17]

Different strains of disease-causing *E. coli* work in different ways. O157 attaches to the wall of the intestine. There it produces a poison that makes the intestine bleed. In children and the elderly, the infection can progress to kidney failure. The Centers for Disease Control in Atlanta record about 73,000 cases of infection and 60 deaths from *E. coli* each year.[18] Washing fruits and vegetables well with water removes *E. coli*. Cooking meats thoroughly and pasteurizing milk and juices kill the bacteria. Hamburger should be cooked to an internal temperature of 160° F or higher.

What Can I Do to Prevent Food Poisoning? Some steps are obvious. Cook hot foods really hot. Keep cold foods really cold. Keep cooking tools and work surfaces clean. Scrub cutting boards with disinfectants; *Salmonella* can survive in them for weeks! Use clean towels and cooking utensils. Cover foods. Don't let juices from thawing meat drip into salads. Pay attention to "use by" dates. Don't eat anything that looks or smells "off." Don't eat food if you "don't know where it's been" or how it's been handled.

But the single most effective measure may surprise you. Wash your hands! Wash them frequently and well, especially before eating, during cooking, and after using the toilet. Why? Because most pathogens get into food through the fecal-oral route. (Yes, that means just what it sounds like!) You may not think you carry any "bad bugs," but chances are, you do. As many as one in ten of us carries *Listeria* in our intestines, and that's only one "bad bug."

Does hand washing make a difference? When Australian researchers worked with staff and children in a day-care center to promote hand washing, episodes of diarrhea dropped by two-thirds.[19]

Are Raw Eggs Safe to Eat? Have you ever noticed the warning on egg cartons reminding you to refrigerate raw eggs and cook them thoroughly before eating? About 1 in every 10,000 eggs produced in the northeastern United States contains *Salmonella* (see previous question).[20] Infection rates are lower in other parts of the country, but the possibility of contamination is always there. The pathogens live harmlessly in the ovaries of an otherwise healthy hen. They are incorporated into some of the eggs she lays.

Once in the human digestive tract, *Salmonella* organisms multiply. They bring on diarrhea, fever, abdominal cramps, headache, nausea, and vomiting. Healthy adults usually recover quickly. *Salmonella* poisoning poses a more serious threat to infants, the elderly, and people with weakened immune systems, such as AIDS patients and people who have had organ transplants.

Salmonella illnesses from raw eggs reached a peak of 3.6 cases per 100,000 people in 1996 and dropped to 2.2 in 1998.[21] Eggs aren't always to blame. One outbreak occurred when the tapioca cooker in a restaurant wasn't heating the pudding hot enough to kill *Salmonella*.

Cooking destroys *Salmonella*, so the only eggs you need to avoid are those with runny yolks or foods made with raw eggs such as homemade eggnog and some salad dressings. Unbaked, homemade cookie dough poses a risk, but the commercial varieties are safe. They contain pasteurized eggs.

Are Raw Oysters Safe to Eat? For many a serious gourmet, oysters on the half shell are a delight. The delight diminishes, however, at the thought of pathogens lying in wait. *Vibrio* and certain other bacteria get into filter-feeding shellfish that live in sewage-polluted water. The bacteria concentrate in the tissue of the shellfish. Cooking destroys them, but they can survive in raw or undercooked foods. When they get into the human gut, they begin to multiply. Their numbers can rise to billions in hours.

Travelers in countries lacking clean water should beware. So should consumers of shellfish harvested along America's coasts. The number of *Vibrio* organisms found in the water increases when the water gets warm. That's why the old advice to avoid shellfish in months without an "r" remains wise today.

Vibrio isn't the only danger. In 2000, Lynn Joens and John Mare at the University of Arizona tested shellfish from both East and West coasts. They found *Salmonella* in 50 to 70 percent and *Campylobacter* in 10 to 15 percent. "Most states test the water, but only for *E. coli*," Joens says.[22] Commercial oyster farms use periodic water changes in tanks to get rid of *E. coli*, but the procedure doesn't eliminate other pathogens in oysters.

Are Food Additives Safe? The answer depends on the additive in question, the state of current research, and the source of the answer. Some researchers and interest groups define safety in different ways. The additive considered safe today may prove dangerous tomorrow, and vice versa.

It's not always easy to tell what an additive is from its name. For example, alginate sounds risky, but isn't. It's a thickening agent taken from seaweed. Alginate keeps ice cream, cheese, candy, and yogurt creamy. Its cousin, the even more deadly sounding propylene glycol alginate, thickens salad dressings and keeps beer from being too foamy—all quite safely.

Other food additives with tongue-twister names are actually beneficial. Ascorbic acid is actually vitamin C. It prevents fruits from turning brown in air. Alpha tocopherol is another name for vitamin E. It keeps oily foods from turning rancid. Not all artificial colorings are risky either. Beta-carotene is used to color margarines. The body converts it to vitamin A. All three additives are antioxidants that combat both heart disease and cancer.

Some additives make food safer. For example, the machines used in food processing can add trace amounts of metals to food. The additive EDTA (for ethylenediamine tetraacetic acid) traps metal impurities, preventing spoilage and discoloration.

Some substances safe for most people may be risky to certain individuals. For example, most people can safely enjoy the flavor enhancer MSG (monosodium glutamate). But for those who are allergic, the result of ingesting even a small amount can bring on "Chinese restaurant syndrome." Its symptoms include headache, dizziness, chest pains, and a tingling or burning sensation on the skin.

On the other hand, some of the most innocent-sounding additives bear watching. Sugar comes in many guises: corn syrup, dextrose, glucose, corn sugar, modified food starch, invert sugar, lactose, monoglycerides, diglycerides, and more. While there's nothing dangerous about sugar itself, too much rots teeth and may pile on unwanted pounds, while displacing nutrient-rich foods from the diet. Many foods contain too much salt (sodium chloride). This safe food additive is risky for people with high blood pressure.

None of this should make you afraid of the foods you eat, but it should prompt you to become a careful label reader. Perhaps it will persuade you to buy fewer "convenience foods" and spend more time in the fresh produce aisle.

Why Do They Put Caffeine in Soft Drinks? Manufacturers say they put caffeine in their fizzy drinks for flavor. Are they right? Johns Hopkins researchers say no. They asked 55 people to taste decaffeinated colas and colas containing six different concentrations of caffeine. Only two of the people could reliably tell the difference between caffeinated and caffeine-free colas. At higher concentrations, most people could taste the caffeine, but they described it as bitter and medicinal. "It is more likely that the stimulant properties of caffeine—rather than the flavor enhancing properties—lead to high rates of soft drinks being consumed in the U.S.," says Roland Griffiths, one of the scientists who conducted the study.[23]

Americans drink 14 billion gallons (about 52 billion liters) of soft drinks annually. That's more than twice the amount manufactured in 1974 and nearly ten times the 1942 production.[24] Caffeine is addictive. Six of the seven most popular soft drinks contain caffeine.[25]

Can Hormones in Animal Foods Affect People? This is a good question that lacks a simple answer. The pituitary glands of cows produce hormones naturally, but farmers and ranchers give nature a boost by supplementing their herds with hormones. Bovine growth hormone or bovine somatotropin

(BGH or bST—not to be confused with "mad cow" disease, BSE) increases milk production in dairy herds by as much as 10 percent.[26] In beef cattle, hormone supplements produce leaner carcasses and lower-fat meat. In the United States, growth hormones are used in 63 percent of all cattle.[27]

The hormones show up in milk and meat, but "residue levels of these hormones in food have been demonstrated to be safe and well below any level that would have an effect on humans," says the FDA.[28] Since 1985, the agency has allowed the marketing of dairy products from BGH-supplemented cows. In 1991, the National Institutes of Health agreed that the milk was safe. The American Medical Association added its approval in 1993.

Despite these assurances, some consumer advocates continue to raise objections—not always for health reasons. Some who oppose BGH say that increased production lowers prices, which is not good for farmers. They say that BGH milk contains more body cells from cows, so it spoils faster.

In addition, some evidence suggests that BGH supplements increase the number of udder infections in dairy herds. That translates into more antibiotics being used to treat sick animals. Critics say that this leads to the growing number of antibiotic-resistant infections found in both humans and cattle.

Hormone-enhanced meat and milk are sold widely in the United States. In most places, no special labeling is required. The situation is different in Europe, where mistrust of hormones runs high. The European Union banned imported meat from hormone-treated animals in 1985. In 1995 a scientific conference held in Brussels concluded that five animal growth hormones pose no risk to human health. Nevertheless, the European Union renewed its ban in 2000.

When ionizing radiation (gamma rays, electron beams, or X rays) passes through food, it kills insects and microorganisms that cause spoilage or disease. The food never comes into contact with radioactive materials, nor does it become radioactive. Irradiation improves food hygiene and lengthens shelf life, says the U.S. Department of Agriculture.

Critics counter that irradiation destroys nutrients in foods, including vitamins B_1, C, and E. Some have suggested that irradiation might

Sterilizing fruit
by radiation
in the laboratory

form free radicals or cancer-causing substances in food, but evidence is scant. American consumers haven't rushed to buy irradiated foods, perhaps because of fear of the word. You may find foods labeled "cold pasteurized" or "electronic pasteurized" in your supermarket. That's irradiated food by another name.

Are Herbal Supplements Safe? The Dietary Supplement and Health Education Act passed by Congress in 1994 allows manufacturers to market "food supplements" without demonstrating either safety or effectiveness. The bill gives consumers more freedom in making health decisions. Along with that freedom comes the responsibility to know the risks and act prudently.

Some say that herbs such as St. John's wort fight the blues. Ginseng, cocoa, and maté are touted as energizers. Varying claims are made for motherwort, echinacea, chamomile, lavender, passionflower, wild cherry, and many others. While some claims may turn out to be genuine, it's wise to guard both your health and your bank account with a dose of healthy skepticism. "Not since the early 1900s," writes journalist Amanda Spake, "have so many bought so much with so little sound science behind it."[29]

Herbal supplements are drugs. All drugs have side effects. Just because they are sold over-the-counter is no guarantee that they will do what they claim to do or be totally safe. Patients should tell their doctors about any herbs or supplements they are taking. Says researcher Ed Robinson of the University of California, Irvine: "Natural does not mean safe. Many natural compounds are toxic."[30]

On the plus side, herbal remedies have a long history of successful use. Garlic, for example, was described as medicinal on clay tablets dating from 2000 B.C. In China, herbal treatments are the basis of family medical practice, as they are in much of Africa and South America today. Although strict laboratory testing and clinical trials are rare for herbal medicines, more research is under way. In 1999 and 2000, the National Institutes of Health established centers for research on medicinal plants in Arizona, Indiana, California, and Illinois. Americans can also obtain information about herbs and supplements through the National Center for Complementary and Alternative Medicine in Silver Spring, Maryland.

For most herbs, research to determine a safe dose has yet to be completed. The strength of herbal preparations varies from one manufacturer to another. Potency can also vary between batches prepared in different places or during different seasons. Interactions with other drugs, foods, herbs, or supplements aren't always known. Some herbs have made headlines for dangerous side effects arising from impurities. Some deaths are attributed to them. "These products are really modern-day snake oil," says Bruce Silverglade of the Center for Science in the Public Interest.[31] "Users are playing roulette with their own bodies," says *Consumer Reports*.[32] For more on herbal supplements, see Table 4 on page 152.

Should I Use Over-the-Counter Appetite Suppressants or Herbs If I Want to Lose Weight? No. Such products have a notorious history. There's no reason to believe that new concoctions will fare any better.

One good example is PPA. On December 6, 2000, the FDA issued a Public Heath Advisory. They asked manufacturers of over-the-counter products containing phenylpropanolamine (PPA) to discontinue the manufacture and marketing of those products. PPA had been shown to increase the risk of hemorrhagic stroke. (That's the death of nerve cells resulting from bleeding in the brain.) PPA pills claimed to control appetite, although many doctors doubted they worked. Alternatives to PPA are available now. You'll probably find them on your drugstore shelves. Until solid evidence proves them both safe and effective, pass them by.

What's Organic Food?

By the chemist's definition, all food is "organic," which simply means carbon-based. The word, however, means something else at the grocery store. Organic farmers cultivate their crops without using artificial pesticides and chemical fertilizers. Organic meats and dairy products come from animals raised on "natural" feed. They are usually vaccinated against disease, but they are given no artificial hormones, growth accelerators, or antibiotics.

In 2000, the U.S. Department of Agriculture announced a national standard for the labeling of organic foods. Labels assure consumers that organic foods are actually grown under the conditions they expect and pay for. Irradiated and genetically modified foods cannot be labeled as organic.

Organic foods are expensive. Some people consider them worth the price, believing that foods grown "the old-fashioned way" are healthier, safer, and more flavorful. "The term 'organic' is a marketing term," says the National Food Processors Association, "not an indicator of quality or safety."[33] Consumers disagree. Seven in every ten food shoppers think that organic food is better for their health.[34]

In one of three ways:

1. **Artificial selection or selective breeding.** This is the same process as the natural selection that drives evolutionary change. However, people—not nature—do the selecting. From a genetically varied population of plants or animals, breeders choose individuals with desirable traits, such as resistance to insects or drought. These become the parent plants for the next generation. It's easy to do in most plants. Take the sperm-containing pollen from the anther of a flower and put it into the female pistil, which contains the ovary and eggs. The seeds that result may grow into a plant that carries the same desirable traits as its parents. Many types of corn, wheat, and other grains were bred this way.

2. **Crossbreeding.** Two strains of the same species may be bred in hopes of producing a new variant that combines positive characteristics from both. Crossbreeding produced the new "super-broccoli." It's the offspring of ordinary broccoli and a scrawny Sicilian relative. It contains a hundred times more sulphoraphane than regular broccoli.[35] This substance causes the body to make enzymes that protect cells against cancer-causing chemicals. It should be noted that this development was not the "hit-or-miss" crossbreeding experiment of old. English scientists used DNA fingerprinting to find the perfect strains for the cross.

3. **Genetic modification** (Also called genetic engineering, transgenic engineering, genetic alteration, gene technology, biotechnology, and recombinant DNA technology.) Genetic modification of crop plants involves moving genes from one species to another. Genes may be transferred to a plant from a bacterium, another plant, or even an animal. Nature doesn't do that, and neither do traditional breeding techniques. The method is a shortcut to developing strains that resist disease or insects, survive weed-killing chemicals, produce higher yields, grow faster, or tolerate salty soils or drought.

Genetic modification of a crop plant requires five steps:

1. transferring the desired gene from the cells of one species to another;

2. growing the plant to see if it contains the transplanted gene;

3. checking to see that the gene works as expected;

4. determining that the gene passes intact from parent to offspring during normal plant reproduction; and

5. testing for environmental and food safety.

Two methods are used to introduce genes into plants. The "cut-and-paste" method relies on the natural ability of *Agrobacterium*, a microorganism that lives naturally in soil, to insert its genes into plant cells. Scientists add desirable genes to the bacterium, and it does the rest. The other method is the "gene gun." Tiny particles of gold or tungsten are coated with DNA from one organism and "fired" into plant tissue of another. The heavy metal particles pass through the cell, but some of the DNA drops off and stays behind. Once inserted and active, the DNA directs the cell to make a particular protein. To do this, genes must be linked to promoters, pieces of DNA that act as switches, essentially "turning them on."

The United States has become the world's leader in the production of genetically modified crop plants. Soybeans and corn are most popular, followed by cotton and canola. Genetically modified plants now cover one-fourth of U.S. cropland.[36]

Is Genetic
Modification
(GM) of Foods
Necessary,
Wise, and
Safe?

After four decades of studying plant disease, R. James Cook at Washington State University welcomes biotechnology. Transplanted genes give plants natural defenses, he says. He hopes to genetically modify barley to resist a deadly root disease. He wonders how the public will react to his research if he is successful. Some people, he says, worry about possible harm of genetically modified crops to humans, animals, or the environment. Will genetically modified crops induce allergies? Can a transplanted gene jump into other species and upset the natural balance of ecosystems?

While scientists and consumers ask whether genetic modification will cause long-range health or environmental problems, others worry that unnecessary fears will hold back progress that might feed the world's hungry. "Millions of Africans—far too many of them children—are suffering from malnutrition and hunger," wrote Nigeria's Agriculture Minister Hassan Adamu in the *Washington Post*. "Agricultural technology offers a way to stop the suffering."[37]

Plants aren't the only genetically modified organisms. This "Enviropig," developed in Canada, carries mouse genes that cause it to excrete less phosphorus in its feces. That reduces the pollution from farm runoff.

It should come as no surprise that people disagree. Here are some of the arguments:

THE PROS	THE CONS
GM foods are cheaper and easier to grow, They damage the environment less because fewer pesticides and herbicides are used to grow them.	GM foods could prove unsafe for human consumption, having unpredicted negative effects on health.
GM foods can be made healthier, for example with greater vitamin or antioxidant content.	GM foods might cause allergies or trigger allergic reactions in already susceptible individuals.
GM foods can vaccinate children against disease in countries where other vaccines are too expensive or too difficult to distribute.	GM decreases the genetic diversity of plant populations, so that they may lose their natural ability to adapt to changing environmental conditions.
GM crops can grow more food on the land now being tilled, so that more land (such as the rain forests of South America and the savannas of Africa) can be preserved.	Transplanted genes can move from one species to another outside human control and cause unexpected, negative consequences, such as herbicide-resistant weed species or pesticide-resistant insects.
GM crops can be grown on land that is too salty, too dry, or too lacking in nutrients to support traditional food crops.	GM plants could harm or kill animals, such as the bees and butterflies that pollinate them.
GM produces the same results as traditional breeding, only more quickly and reliably.	GM could unintentionally decrease nutrients in foods or increase toxins.
GM foods will feed the world's growing and hungry population, expected to grow another 1.5 billion by 2020.[38]	It's morally wrong for agricultural companies to patent crops and force farmers to buy seed from them.

What's Eaten, But Isn't Food?

· · · ·

At twelve, she began to have the Green Sickness: and became very feeble, weak, lean, pale, and short breathed. She eat Chalk, Plaster, Earth, and Coals; but had little inclination to any natural Diet. She had a great Gnawing and Pain in her Stomach; which the Chalk and other Things mitigated, and asswaged for the Time.

PHYSICIAN JOHN WOODWARD'S ACCOUNT OF A PATIENT (1757)

· · · ·

Name something that people eat that is not food. If you answered ashes, balloons, chalk, metal, grass, crayons, insects, sand, soap, paste, string, baby powder, or paint chips, read no further. You are already an expert on geophagia (clay eating), pagophagia (ice eating), and other forms of pica—or eating things that aren't foods.

Pica gets its name from the Latin word for magpie. Magpies eat just about anything, but humans who eat nonfoods are choosier. The compulsion usually focuses on a single item.

Doctors have operated on people whose intestines were blocked with nuts, bolts, or screws. People who regularly consume twigs, newsprint, or bathroom deodorizers are not as rare as you might guess.

Pica is defined, in part, by cultural norms. In the United States today, eating clay is considered pica, but in past centuries it was not. Clay eating and soil eating were common in the 1800s, especially among slaves in the South. In the 1950s and 1960s, the practice was so popular that clay-filled lunch bags were sold

Bags of clay are sold as snack foods in convenience stores and roadside markets in the southern United States.

at Alabama bus stops as snacks for travelers. Southerners mailed bags of hometown clay to their friends and relatives who moved north. Some reports estimate that clay eating is a daily practice in more than two hundred cultures worldwide.[39]

Some pica behaviors involve substances that are foods but are not usually eaten alone or in large quanti-ties. For example, small amounts of cornstarch thicken gravies and fruit pies. People with amylophagia may eat two or three boxes of cornstarch a week. Ingesting one-half box or more of cornstarch daily releases enough sugar into the bloodstream to send blood glucose levels rocketing. That can trigger diabetes, especially in pregnant women.

Why do people eat nonfood substances? In some cultures, pica is practiced for medicinal purposes and may actually have some value. For example, people in some parts of Nigeria eat kaolinite (a form of clay) to combat diarrhea. The clay forms a protective coating in the lining of the intestine and binds bacteria there, thus relieving diarrhea.

Other people say they eat clay, starch, or some other substance simply because they enjoy the taste, texture, or smell. Others claim pica behavior—such as crunching the frost that collects in the freezer— eases tension and anxiety. Some pregnant women eat clay because they believe it will relieve morning sickness. Some mental-health professionals categorize pica as an obsessive-compulsive disorder. This term describes people who feel powerless to stop a behavior they know is bizarre, even risky.

Doctors can't always tell whether their patients are consuming nonfoods. People don't tell, either because they are embarrassed or because they see nothing odd about it. To find out how common pica truly is, Ellen Simpson and her colleagues in California asked pregnant Hispanic women about their eating habits. Somewhere between a third and a half reported eating nonfood items. Their favorites included dirt, ashes, clay, and magnesium carbonate, a mineral sold in blocks in Mexican pharmacies as a laxative. Some of the women said they simply liked the taste, texture, or aroma of the nonfood substances. Others said they "couldn't help themselves."

Most thought that the pica was good for them or for the babies they carried. They believed that failure to satisfy their pica cravings would lead to miscarriage, illness, or an unhappy baby. The researchers could find no particular pattern in pica preferences. "Women who ate tar lived next door to women who ate laundry bluing who lived next door to women who ate dirt."[40]

Doctors worry less about the pica itself than about its outcomes. Serious consequences include:

- poisoning, such as lead poisoning from eating chips of old paint or soil that has old paint in it;

- obstruction of the bowel or airways from consuming or choking on indigestible materials such as hair;

- obesity from consuming too many calories—for example, eating laundry starch;

- inadequate protein or energy intake from consuming things like coffee grounds or oyster shells in place of real foods;

- nutritional deficiencies, such as the interference of soil with the absorption of iron, zinc, and potassium in the digestive system;

- damage to teeth and gums from chewing abrasive materials such as twigs or metals;

- infestations of parasites such as tapeworms resulting from consuming dirt or feces;

- high blood pressure, high levels of sodium salts in the blood, and abnormal liver functions such as those resulting from consuming large quantities of baking powder;

- low birth weight, premature birth, mental and physical abnormalities, and even death among infants whose mothers practice pica during pregnancy.

Doctors debate whether nutritional deficiencies cause pica. For example, much research has established a link between ice eating and iron deficiency. In some studies, treatment with iron supplements reduced or eliminated ice eating. That fact suggests that the deficiency induced the behavior; but population studies have failed to confirm the hypothesis. People with normal iron levels are as likely to eat ice as those whose iron levels are low.

Some specialists fear that pica is as much of a threat to health today as it was in 1898, when T. C. Allbutt wrote: "The appetite . . . is often marked by caprices and perversions which put serious obstacles in the way of nutrition."

· · · ·

CHAPTER FIVE

ABOUT FOOD
AS MEDICINE

A good kitchen is a good apothecary's shop.

• WILLIAM BULLEIN •

Can Food Be Medicine? "Functional foods," "designer foods," or "nutraceuticals," provide health benefits beyond basic nutrition.[1] They include certain food additives and foods designed for special dietary uses, such as sugar-free foods for people with diabetes. The definition also includes many natural foods. For example, tomatoes are naturally rich in lycopene. Diets high in lycopene reduce the risk of prostate and cervical cancers.

Some functional foods are enriched or fortified with added vitamins, minerals, or phytochemicals.[2] ("Phyto" means "plant.") "Improving" on natural food is nothing new. Milk in the United States has been a functional food since the 1930s when dairies first began adding vitamin D. More recently, some companies have begun adding calcium to

Functional foods are nothing new. This ad for Ovaltine appeared in a magazine called *Holland's* in March 1947.

orange juice, pasta, and rice. Many chocolate drink mixes are vitamin/mineral pills in a powder.

Do Pregnant Women Need Extra Vitamins and Minerals?

Yes, and many doctors prescribe them. One especially important vitamin for all women is folic acid or folate. Folate forms a part of the enzymes cells use to make DNA. Without it, cells cannot divide. A folate deficiency in a pregnant woman can cause a serious birth defect in her child. The damage is done often before the woman even knows she's pregnant.

How does this happen? Between the third and fourth weeks of pregnancy, the neural tube forms in the embryo. Sheets of cells fold inward, becoming a U-shaped groove. Then the edges move together and fuse into the neural tube. The fetal brain and spinal cord develop from it. Without folate, the tube does not join properly. The result may be as severe as anencephaly (failure of the brain to form). More often, spina bifida, the failure of the spine to close, produces paralysis or retardation.[3]

Because as many as half of all pregnancies are unplanned, every female who menstruates should eat foods rich in folate and consider taking a folic acid supplement. The human body neither makes nor stores folate, so adequate amounts are needed in the diet daily. Foods rich in folate include leafy green vegetables, oranges, peanuts, and beans.

For many years, the annual rate of spina bifida in the United States hovered around 2,500.[4] In 1998 government regulation mandated the addition of folate to flour, breads, cereals, and pastas. By the year 2000, the number of babies born with defects of the neural tube had dropped by nearly 20 percent.[5] Greater progress is possible. Girls and women "need to take a multivitamin containing folic acid every day before [they] get pregnant," says Jennifer L. Howse, president of the March of Dimes Birth Defect Foundation.[6]

Can Certain Brands of Margarine and Salad Dressing Reduce Cholesterol?

Some of them can, and the National Institutes of Health advises their use along with a fat-controlled diet, exercise, and weight control for people who need to reduce their levels of blood cholesterol. Lowering blood cholesterol levels can help prevent heart disease.

Margarines and salad dressings that claim to reduce cholesterol work because they contain plant compounds called stanols. Stanols are made from wood pulp, soybean oil, or tall oil (a by-product of making paper from pine trees). In margarines and salad dressings, the stanols are processed with fatty acids from vegetable oils to form compounds called stanol esters. Stanol esters can lower total cholesterol and LDL ("bad" cholesterol) by 10 to 15 percent.[7] They can prevent the cholesterol in food from crossing the wall of the small intestine and entering the blood. Both the stanols and the cholesterol are eliminated in feces. Since stanols are not absorbed, they are thought to be safe. No studies have shown that the esters interfere with the absorption of fat-soluble vitamins. "As part of a low-fat diet, [these margarines] reduce . . . total cholesterol and LDL concentrations significantly," says Finnish scientist M. A. Hallikainen.[8] And they seem to work just as well in people with mildly elevated cholesterol as in those with severe cases.

Can Soybeans Prevent Heart Attacks? As a substitute for animal protein, soy can cut risks of heart disease in people with high levels of blood cholesterol. In some studies, soy reduced total cholesterol and LDLs by about 10 percent while increasing HDLs by 4 percent or more.[9]

"Soy itself is not a magic food," says Christine Lewis of the FDA, "but it . . . can have a positive effect on health."[10] It reduces the blood's level of oxidized cholesterol. That form of cholesterol is taken up rapidly by artery walls, forming plaques that block blood flow to the heart muscle. Soy may have other benefits. Some experts think that it may help prevent osteoporosis (brittle bones), memory loss in older people, and some kinds of cancers.[11]

Yes. In the 1930s scientists noticed a trend. Where fluoride levels were high in the water supply, people had fewer cavities. Research in the years that followed confirmed a cause-and-effect relationship: Add fluoride to the water and watch tooth decay decline. At the turn of the twentieth century, most people expected to lose their natural teeth by midlife. By the turn of the twenty-first, "false teeth" were a curiosity of the past, at least for the young.

Fluoride works by promoting the natural process of "remineralization." Teeth contain calcium phosphate. Fluoride ions (charged particles) replace hydroxyl ions (charged molecules of oxygen and hydrogen), forming the acid-resistant substance fluorapatite. The calcium and phosphate in saliva enter teeth more readily when fluorapatite is present.

Good eating reduces risks slightly, but "the [cancer-causing] effect of smoking is so big," says scientist Stephanie London, "that it is not going to even come close to wiping out the smoking effect."[12]

London studied 18,000 men in China, where many smoke and cancer rates are high. Over ten years, the men who had the highest levels of isothiocyanates in their blood were slightly less likely to develop cancer, whether they smoked or not. Isothiocyanates are antioxidants. They are found in vegetables such as broccoli, cabbage, cauliflower, and bok choy. The study showed that inheritance plays a part. Men whose bodies broke down isothiocyanates were more likely to develop cancer.[13]

London's work begs the question: "Can smokers pop a pill and escape lung cancer?" Isothiocyanates are not available in pill form, but they wouldn't be a good idea anyway. Researchers don't know how the more than 20 different kinds of isothiocyanates interact with each other. Studies with vitamin A have shown that too much actually increases cancer risk. The same might prove true for isothiocyanates. "The lesson," London says, "is 'just eat the vegetables.'" And, of course, don't smoke.

Does Food Affect Emotions and Mood?

"What we eat affects our memory, mood, and vitality long before it affects our heart and bones," says Elizabeth Somer, author of *Food and Mood*.[14] Skipping meals and loading up on sugar and caffeine can generate negative moods. Healthy food choices can have positive effects, she says.

How? The answer may lie in the chemistry of the brain and nervous system. Nerve impulses carry messages from the environment to the brain and vice versa. Molecules called neurotransmitters are chemical messengers. They transmit a nerve impulse across the gap between nerve cells. The release of neurotransmitter molecules from one neuron and their attachment to receptor sites on the next keep a nerve impulse moving.

"Many neurotransmitters are built from the foods we eat," says neuroscientist Eric Chudler of the University of Washington.[15] If the diet is deficient in raw materials, then the brain cannot produce the neurotransmitters it uses to send messages and make memories. For example, vitamin C from orange juice, tomatoes, cabbage, and potatoes helps make serotonin. Serotonin affects the walls of blood vessels, influences moods, and promotes sleep. It may also produce feelings of calmness, relaxation, and contentment. Drugs that prevent its reuptake (into the neuron that released it) are prescribed to treat depression. In at least some healthy, nondepressed people, carbohydrate foods seem to enhance serotonin production and produce similar effects. "It is the balance between different neurotransmitters that helps regulate mood," Chudler says.[16]

Are There Any Foods That Can't Be Eaten When Taking Certain Medicines? Yes. Ask your pharmacist about interactions when you get a prescription filled. One food to avoid with many drugs is grapefruit juice. It blocks an enzyme in the intestine that breaks down the drugs. As a result, too much drug is absorbed into the bloodstream. Medicines that are too potent can have unexpected side effects, says Garvan Kane of the Mayo Clinic.[17]

Are There Any Herbs That Shouldn't Be Taken Together or With Other Medicines? Yes, and the lists are long. For example, the herb kava is made into a tea that some people drink to relax. It should not be taken with sedatives, sleeping pills, antipsychotic drugs, alcohol, antidepressants, drugs used to treat Parkinson's disease, or anesthetics used during surgery. Echinacea, which some people think boosts the immune system, should not be taken with steroid drugs. St. John's wort, used for mild depression, shouldn't be combined with prescription drugs, particularly antidepressants. Because laxatives can speed up the absorption of herbs and other drugs, they should not be taken at the same time either.

"The problem is that many people don't consider herbal preparations medicines. But, in fact, they are, because they contain active ingredients," says anesthesiologist Michael Jakubowski.[18] Always tell your doctor if you are taking any food supplement, herbal preparation, or vitamin—no matter how harmless you may think it is.

Should I Take Creatine and Protein Supplements to Build Muscles?

The idea that these supplements might prove valuable grew out of studies of normal muscle growth and action. Muscles are made of protein, and the body produces creatine as an energy source for muscles. Creatine is used quickly in sports that require short bursts of intense activity, such as sprinting or bench pressing. Doctors say creatine doesn't increase muscle size on its own, but it does work for some professional athletes who are training for long hours daily. Studies are needed to determine its safety. No one knows its risks for young people, although some cases of serious muscle pain and dehydration (loss of water) have been reported. Until more is known, pass the creatine supplements by.

As for protein supplements, they probably aren't necessary. A normal, balanced diet provides adequate protein. How much is enough? Researchers recommend about 1 gram daily per kilogram (2.2 pounds) of body weight. For a 150-pound (68-kilogram) teen, that's about 68 grams (2.3 ounces), or the amount contained in a skinless chicken breast and a cup of lowfat yogurt.

Is Fish Considered Brain Food?

Fish has long been praised as "brain food," but no single food can make such a claim, says neuroscientist Eric Chudler. "Certainly fish contains many nutrients that are essential for proper brain function. But I don't know of any evidence that shows eating fish every day will turn you into a genius."[19]

Proper nutrition, however, may indeed enhance brainpower. Choline is a substance similar to the B vitamins. It's found in egg yolks, whole wheat, peanuts, milk, green peas, liver, beans, seafood, and soybeans. The brain uses it to make the neurotransmitter acetylcholine. To test the effects of choline on memory and learning, researchers at the Massachusetts Institute of Technology gave memory tests to college students before increasing the amount of choline in their subjects' diets. Later, they retested. On the average, memories were better, and the students learned a list of unrelated words more easily.

The Doctor Told Me to Eat Yogurt After I Finish Taking All My Antibiotics. Why?

Antibiotics kill bacteria—all of them!—even the "friendly" ones that work in the normal, healthy intestine. Antibiotics also kill the beneficial bacteria that form a barrier against infection by pathogens. Eating yogurt helps replace the good bacteria you need. Just make sure the yogurt label reads "active culture"—meaning the bacteria in the yogurt are still alive.

What Health Claims Are Food Manufacturers Allowed To Make?

You'll see more claims in advertising than on labels. That's because the Federal Trade Commission has more lenient rules for advertising than the Food and Drug Administration has for labeling.

The table opposite shows some of the labeling claims allowed by the FDA based on scientific evidence. The number will grow.

How to read the table: The arrows pointing up ↑ mean "increase." The arrows pointing down ↓ mean "decrease." So, for example, the first entry means, "Increasing calcium in the diet reduces the risk of osteoporosis.

Diet	Risk
↑ calcium	↓ osteoporosis
↓ total fat	↓ some cancers
↓ saturated fat and cholesterol	↓ heart disease
↑ fiber, fruits, and vegetables	↓ heart disease
↑ fiber, fruits, and vegetables	↓ some cancers
↓ sodium (salt)	↓ high blood pressure
↑ folic acid	↓ neural tube defects (in babies)
↓ sugar	↓ cavities in teeth
↑ soluble fiber (as in oatmeal) along with a fat-controlled diet	↓ heart disease
↑ soy protein (to 25 grams a day) along with a fat-controlled diet	↓ heart disease

How Important Is Diet in Cancer Prevention?

The American Institute for Cancer Research says one dietary change could prevent as many as 20 percent of all cancers.[20] What is that change? Eat at least five servings of fruits and vegetables daily. The Institute recommends the "New American Plate." It's two-thirds (or more) plant foods and one-third (or less) animal foods.

Does Garlic Prevent Cancer or Heart Disease? Experts disagree. In October 2000, the *American Journal of Clinical Nutrition* published a review of 22 research projects. The authors concluded that "people who consume raw or cooked garlic regularly face about half the risk of stomach cancer and two-thirds the risk of colorectal cancer as people who eat little or none."[21] They found, however, no benefit from garlic supplements.

That same month, the Agency for Healthcare Research and Quality published their report. "The evidence was inconclusive about garlic's role in protecting against cancer," the agency said.[22] They stated that garlic may help reduce LDLs and triglycerides in the short term (one to three months), but not beyond that. They found no benefit of garlic for high blood pressure or diabetes either.

Are Drugs Ever Made From Food? "Nearly half of all medicines in use today come directly from plants (or fungal or bacterial sources) or have been adapted chemically from a plant molecule," says Ed Robinson, a research scientist at the University of California, Irvine.[23] His work reveals how new drugs are located and developed from plants, many of them foods.

More than a decade ago, anthropologist Joe Bastien told Robinson that the Kallawaya Indians in Bolivia use extracts from green coffee beans to treat a variety of common illnesses. Following up on that tip, Robinson and his team isolated a compound called L-chicoric acid from unroasted beans. Remarkably, they found that the substance blocks an enzyme that HIV (the virus that causes AIDS) uses to infect blood cells.

Although the acid is not potent enough to stop AIDS by itself, Robinson hopes it can someday be used in combination with other anti-AIDS drugs. He is working to synthesize analogues—molecules that are similar to, yet distinct from, L-chicoric acid. An analogue might turn out to be safer and more effective. Robinson isn't stopping with L-chicoric acid. He has tested more than 60 Bolivian plants and found several that act against HIV. He is also studying plants from Pakistan and China. Some, he thinks, look promising.

Does Nutrition Affect the Immune System?

"Worldwide, the most common cause of immuno-deficiency is malnutrition," writes Steve Bunk in *The Scientist*.[24] Poor nutrition plays a major role in the body's susceptibility to infections. Evidence is strong that it has a role in pneumonia, measles, and tuberculosis, Bunk says. The effect of poor nutrition on other diseases, such as flu and AIDS, may be weaker.

How Can Foods Work as Vaccines?

A vaccine is any substance that causes the recipient to build up antibodies against it. Most vaccines use whole organisms—live, weakened, or dead—to do that. Now researchers are getting the same effect with a single protein from a disease-causing microbe. For example, an edible form of a hepatitis B vaccine uses a protein from the hepatitis virus to trigger the immune response.

Edible vaccines have many advantages. Those that protect against cholera and dysentery could be genetically engineered into cheap, tasty foods such as bananas and could save the lives of millions of children in developing countries. Vaccines that use whole organisms require cold storage. Edible vaccines do not. That makes distribution easier and cheaper for third world nations.

What Can Be Done to Feed Hungry People in Today's World?

Hunger is a reality worldwide. In the Unites States, where about 100 billion pounds (450 billion kilograms) of food goes to waste every year, 31 million people are hungry or at risk.[25] In the year 2008, experts predict, sub-Saharan Africa will contain 25 percent of the world's population. It will also account for 80 percent of what James Shroeder of the U.S. Department of Agriculture calls "the nutrition gap."[26] The gap is the difference between the food supply and people's minimal needs.

Too little food is not the only enemy. Vitamin A deficiency is the leading cause of blindness and death in children in the developing world. More than 250 million children are deficient in vitamin A. (As amazing as it may seem, that number represents a major improvement. The efforts of the United Nation's Children's Emergency Fund, UNICEF, to get vitamin A to mothers and children has cut it by two-thirds since 1980.) Ten million children have xeropthalmia, or "dry eye," and another half million are blind. Three million die annually of complications from measles that could be prevented with vitamin A.[27] How much vitamin A does a child need? Between 400 and 600 micrograms a day. That's about the same as you get by eating just one carrot.

Some world leaders believe that genetic modification is the best hope for feeding millions who are hungry. Relief may come from some unexpected sources. One is the humble sweet potato. In sub-Saharan East Africa, children fill up with a starchy, white-fleshed potato that contains few nutrients. A bright orange sweet potato known as SPK004 has been bred by plant scientists in Peru. It contains many nutrients and is rich in vitamin A. Growing it in Africa could save millions from death and blindness.

Will Food Scientists Ever Settle All Their Disagreements and Recommend the Perfect Diet?

Probably not. Here are a dozen reasons why:

1. *Individual differences.* Individuals differ in their responses to foods or specific nutrients. What happens in 99 people won't necessarily happen in the 100th person, and there's no way to predict the difference.

2. *Expectations.* A change in diet may make a person feel better simply because of the change. When human beings expect an improvement, they usually get it.

3. *Experimental design.* It's difficult for researchers to study a single variable. Adding a food to the diet adds many substances to the diet, not just one. That's why nutritional research is usually done with supplements, but supplements may have effects that real food wouldn't, or vice versa.

4. *Multiple factors.* Poor nutrition isn't the only reason for complaints such as depression or forgetfulness. In human research, scientists try to control for factors such as age, sex, family background, education, social or family status, and other factors, but they can never be entirely successful in identifying and matching all possible influences.

5. *Variable outcomes.* Effects are often a matter of degree. For example, skipping breakfast impairs mental performance, but a large breakfast impairs concentration. For many people, carbohydrate foods are morning energizers but evening relaxers. Isolating and controlling all the variables is tough.

6. *Indefinable outcomes.* The outcomes are hard to define and measure. For example, how does one define memory, mood, or intelligence in order to determine if diet affects them?

7. *Unreliable data.* Self-reports are unreliable. People may give inaccurate medical histories to researchers, either deliberately or unintentionally. If they claim a change because of a diet, who is to say they are right or wrong?

8. *Unreliable instruments.* The questionnaires used to measure dietary habits may be too general or too vague. They may assess what people remember or don't mind reporting, but their accuracy is doubtful. Can you remember exactly what you ate three days ago? Probably not, so how good is your recall for the last five years?

9. *Procedural difficulties.* Some studies ask people to keep diaries of everything they eat. Doing that motivates people to change what they eat so they "look good" on paper. Or it may tempt them into "forgetting" to record a large order of fries or a second piece of pie.

10. *Statistical limitations.* Statistics that predict trends in large populations cannot be used to predict for individuals. For example, risk reduction only applies to large groups. It cannot be applied to any one person in the group.

11. *Limitations of measurement.* Some links between diet and health are so subtle—if they exist at all—that our measurement tools and statistical techniques are too crude to detect them.

12. *Ethical constraints.* The experiments that would settle many issues cannot be done because they are unethical. For example, determining the effects of a dietary deficiency would mean intentionally depriving humans of an essential nutrient. That's morally, ethically, and legally wrong. No responsible researcher would propose such a project, and no research review committee would approve it.

Chicken Soup:
The Ultimate Medicine?

• • • •

Kitchen Physic is the best Physic.

JONATHAN SWIFT

• • • •

You have a cold. The symptoms developed a few days ago, when cold viruses invaded your upper respiratory tract. That led to what researchers call a cytokine cascade. Cytokines are proteins. They are part of the body's disease-fighting response to viral invaders. Cytokines trigger inflammation of the airways. Their cascade is now causing your nose tissues to swell and weep fluid. Your eyes drip. Your breathing passages clog with mucus. You feel miserable. What can help you feel better? Some good old chicken soup!

Chicken soup has been a tried and true remedy throughout history.

The Egyptian physician and philosopher Maimonides wrote the first prescription for chicken soup. He prescribed it in the twelfth century, but he didn't invent the treatment. He got his tip from earlier Greek sources.

It wasn't until the twenty-first century, however, that Nebraska scientists decided to test chicken soup scientifically. They observed the effect of homemade and commercial chicken soups on neutrophils. Neutrophils, the most numerous white cells in the blood, belong to a class of cells called granulocytes. All granulocytes are made in bone marrow. Their granules act as storage depots for infection-fighting chemicals. When releasing those chemical weapons, the granules fuse with the cell membrane. That opens the granule to the outside and causes its contents to spill out.

Cytokines attract neutrophils to the sites of a virus infection. If chicken soup eases cold symptoms, the scientists reasoned, maybe it does it by slowing or blocking neutrophil movement. To test their hypothesis, they collected neutro-phils from the blood of healthy, nonsmoker volunteers. They used chemotaxis chambers to measure neutrophil movement. They put dilutions of various soups in the top and bottom wells of the chambers. They added a serum known to attract neutrophils to the bottom well. They counted the number of cells that moved through a mem-brane between the wells. They expressed their results as the aver-age number of cells found to have

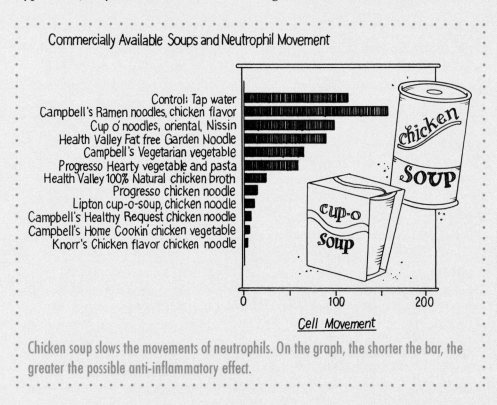

Commercially Available Soups and Neutrophil Movement

Cell Movement

Chicken soup slows the movements of neutrophils. On the graph, the shorter the bar, the greater the possible anti-inflammatory effect.

migrated when examined in the field of a high-power microscope.

In nearly every case, chicken soup reduced the number of neutrophils that moved through a filter toward the attractant. The scientists tested diluted samples of the homemade soup at various stages in its preparation. They found that the vegetables in the soup inhibited neutrophil movement but killed some of the cells. The chicken broth alone and the complete soup slowed migration without killing cells.

Of the 13 supermarket brands they tested, 5 were as good as or better than the homemade soup. Two did nothing. One actually increased neutrophil movement a little. Every experiment needs a control, and the control here was the tap water of Omaha, Nebraska. It had no effect.

The scientists concluded that the anti-inflammatory effect might account for the power of chicken soup to fight the common cold. Or maybe it combats dehydration and provides important nutrients. The comfort factor can't be discounted either. Neither can the "placebo effect." If you expect chicken soup to make you feel better, it probably will.

The research is, as you might guess, controversial.

. . . .

In Closing

What have you thought about as you read the questions and answers on these pages? Perhaps you have come to appreciate the complexity and efficiency of those vital organs inside you—so invisible, yet so essential. Until now, you may have taken them for granted, never giving a thought to how much you rely on them for your very survival. Perhaps you have also come to realize that your digestive system is much more than a simple tube. Its energy release and transfer mechanisms sustain your life. Its structures and working parts organize and distribute the raw materials that build, maintain, and repair everything that is you.

"Looks aren't everything. It's what's inside you that really matters. A biology teacher told me that."

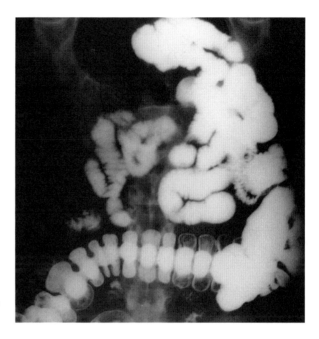

An X ray of the digestive system, showing the esophagus, stomach, duodenum, and small intestine.

Stop for a few seconds today and take a hard look at some food you are about to eat. As you examine that food, think of it as an item for sale in the most elegant jewelry store on Earth. Imagine that you have come to the store to select the perfect gemstone—one of great value that will give you pride and joy for years to come. Is this food you are about to acquire a jewel of the finest quality? Or is it a fake that glitters for the moment, but fails to deliver the everlasting gleam and durability of the real thing? If this "gem" of a food looks dull when studied in this way, consider making another choice. You have nothing to lose. While an exquisite diamond costs a fortune, rich, nutritious foods do not. And their enduring beauty will stay with you for a lifetime.

Take with you the wisdom of the cartoon opposite. As the frog says, "Looks aren't everything. It's what's inside you that counts."

Table 1

SOME IMPORTANT VITAMINS, THEIR FUNCTIONS, AND SOURCES

VITAMIN	FUNCTION	GOOD SOURCES
Vitamin A	Antioxidant: repairs cellular damage caused by free radicals; used in visual pigments in the eyes; important to immune function and skin structure; bone growth; tooth development	Animal foods such as beef liver, egg yolks, butter and cream; also most green and yellow vegetables (carotenoids converted to vitamin A)
Thiamin or Thiamine (B_1)	Regulates functions of nerves and heart; regulates cellular metabolism in getting energy from carbohydrate foods; muscle action, growth and development	Whole grain breads and cereals, pork, salmon, soybeans, beans, liver
Riboflavin (B_2)	Carbohydrate metabolism; membranes lining nose, mouth and stomach; promotes growth; helps break down fat; involved in synthesis of red blood cells and glycogen	Cheese, eggs, chicken, beef, almonds
Pyridoxine (B_6)	Brain function; blood cell formation; maintains chemical balance among bodily fluids; involved in metabolism and many enzyme-catalyzed reactions	Bananas, carrots, fish, nuts, soybeans
Niacin (nicotinic acid or nicotinamide)	Use of sugars and fats in cells; normal function of digestive system; may reduce cholesterol levels	Liver, meat, fish, beans and peas, whole grain cereals
Biotin	Metabolism of carbohydrates and fatty acids	Cauliflower, nuts, peas and beans, kidneys, egg yolks, yeast, liver

DISSOLVES IN	SYMPTOMS OF DEFICIENCY	SYMPTOMS OF EXCESS	NOTES
Fat	Difficulty seeing in dim light; thickening of skin around hair follicles; frequent infections; poor bone growth, weak tooth enamel, weight loss	Headaches; flaking skin; enlargement of the spleen and kidneys; pain in the joints	Milk and flour are fortified with vitamin A in the U. S. and some other countries.
Water	Heart failure; nerve and brain abnormalities	Water soluble: Excess excreted in urine	Cereals are often enriched with thiamin.
Water	Skin irritations; cracks at the corners of the mouth; vision difficulties; inflammation of the tongue; light sensitivity; itching; dizziness; insomnia; slow learning	Water soluble: Excess excreted in urine	Cereals are often enriched with riboflavin.
Water	Deficiency disease not described	Water soluble: Excess excreted in urine	
Water	Abnormalities in brain and intestinal function; skin disorders; ringing in ears; dizziness	Water soluble: Excess excreted in urine	The amino-acid tryptophan can be converted to niacin in the intestine by bacterial action.
Water	Inflammation of the lips and skin; deficiency rare	Water soluble: Excess excreted in urine	

VITAMIN	FUNCTION	GOOD SOURCES
B_{12} (cyanocobalamin)	Red blood cells; nerve function (needed to build the myelin sheath that surrounds nerve fibers); formation of the genetic material DNA; normal growth and development	Meats, eggs, dairy products
Folic acid (folate)	Red blood cells; manufacture of genetic materials DNA and RNA; central nervous system maintenance; promotes growth and development	Leafy green vegetables, fruits, liver, yeast
Vitamin C	Immune system functions; healing of wounds; health of bones and connective tissues (such as tendons and ligaments); elasticity of blood vessels; an antioxidant that repairs cellular damage resulting from the action of free radicals	Oranges, lemons and other citrus fruits; tomatoes, potatoes, cabbage, green peppers
Vitamin D	Absorption of calcium and phosphorus across the intestinal wall; growth, repair, and strength of bones and teeth	Fish liver oils, egg yolks, milk (with vitamin D added); forms in the skin when exposed to the sun's ultraviolet light
Vitamin E (tocopherol)	Antioxidant; forms part of cell membranes	Vegetable oil, wheat germ, egg yolks, margarine, beans and peas, leafy green vegetables, almonds, peanuts
Vitamin K	Blood clotting; absorption of fat across the intestinal wall; may also play a role in calcification of bones	Pork, liver, vegetable oils, leafy vegetables; manufactured by bacteria in the intestine

DISSOLVES IN	SYMPTOMS OF DEFICIENCY	SYMPTOMS OF EXCESS	NOTES
Water	Impaired vision; mental disorders; anemia (in strict vegetarians and people with tapeworms)	Water soluble: Excess excreted in urine	Vegetarians need supplements, but body's stores can last up to five years.
Water	Decrease in number of blood cells; overly large red blood cells; anemia; weakness; lethargy; paleness; mental confusion; headaches	Water soluble: Excess excreted in urine	Supplementation with folic acid is especially important to any girl or woman of reproductive age. It prevents birth defects.
Water	Disorders in the mouth including bleeding, loose teeth, inflammation of gums; stiff joints; bleeding under the skin	Water soluble: Excess excreted in urine	Taking large doses of vitamin C to prevent or treat colds is debated. More research needed.
Fat	Abnormal bone growth and weakness; muscle spasms; rickets	Loss of appetite; nausea and vomiting; weakness; nervousness; thirst; excess urination; kidney failure; calcium deposits throughout the body	Milk is usually fortified with vitamins A and D.
Fat	Rupture of red blood cells; damage to nerves	Causes the body to need more vitamin K	
Fat	Abnormal bleeding; may be caused by treatment with antibiotics or anti-clotting drugs		Treated with injections of vitamin K

Table 2

SOME IMPORTANT MINERALS, THEIR FUNCTIONS, AND SOURCES

MINERAL	FUNCTION	GOOD SOURCES
Sodium	Helps maintain body's acid-base balance; involved in nerve function and muscle action; necessary for the transport of amino acids and glucose into body cells	Salt, meat, cheese, bread, corn, sauerkraut
Chloride	Balance of electrolytes in body fluids and blood; makes stomach acid	Same as sodium (Table salt is sodium chloride.)
Potassium	Used in transmitting nerve impulses and triggering muscle action; helps maintain body's acid-base and water balance; maintains normal blood pressure	Fruits, vegetables, soy flour, beans, salad, nuts, meat, milk
Calcium	Bone and teeth growth and strength; blood clotting; transmission of nerve impulses and initiation of muscle contractions; normal heartbeat rate	Milk and other dairy products, broccoli, sardines, beans
Phosphorus	Building healthy teeth and bones; maintaining the body's acid-base balance; used in making the genetic materials DNA and RNA; forms part of ATP (the energy molecule)	Milk, cheese, meat, chicken and turkey, fish, cereal, nuts, beans, peas
Magnesium	Formation of bones and teeth; nerve impulse transmission; muscle contraction; involved in more than 300 enzyme-catalyzed reactions	Nuts, whole grains, seafood, leafy green vegetables
Iron	Used in some enzymes and in the control of certain chemical reactions; used in building red blood cells and muscle cells	Beef, liver, beans, clams, peaches, soybeans

SYMPTOMS OF DEFICIENCY	SYMPTOMS OF EXCESS	NOTES
Deficiency accompanies dehydration (excessive loss of water); symptoms include mental confusion; loss of appetite; muscle cramps; and vomiting	Confusion and coma; high blood pressure (in one-third to one-half of population)	Most people get more sodium in their diet than they need. Excess sodium can contribute to high blood pressure in some individuals.
Rare; may occur along with excess sodium loss through sweating, vomiting, or diarrhea	Normally, excess excreted in urine. Associated with kidney disease, anemia, heart disease, and pregnancy	
Fatigue; vomiting; swollen abdomen; muscle weakness; paralysis; loss of appetite; low blood pressure; thirst; drowsiness; confusion; coma; high blood pressure	Muscle weakness; low blood pressure; mental confusion; heart attack	Runners often eat bananas during marathons to counteract excess potassium loss in the sweat.
Muscle spasms; bone weakness and brittleness; nerve sensitivity; brittle nails; irritability; palpitations; insomnia	Kidney failure; mental disorders	Requires adequate levels of vitamin D and magnesium for absorption; the most abundant mineral in the body
Muscle weakness; blood cell abnormalities; irritability; malfunctions of kidneys and intestines; loss of appetite; joint pain; stiffness; speech disorders; mental confusion	Calcium and vitamin D deficiencies; may also prevent absorption of iron, magnesium, and zinc	Soft drinks containing high levels of phosphorus interfere with calcium absorption.
Abnormal functions of nerves; anorexia; weakness; fatigue; dizziness; muscle cramps and tremors; low blood sugar and many more	Low blood pressure; failure of the respiratory system; irregular heartbeat rhythms; diarrhea; skin flushing; low blood pressure; loss of reflexes; nausea; shallow breathing	Interacts with calcium in many body processes
Anemia; difficulty swallowing; disturbed sleep; eye inflammation; mouth ulcers; hair loss; intestinal abnormalities; impaired learning and work performance	Deterioration of the gut lining; vomiting; diarrhea; liver damage; abdominal and joint pain; weight loss; excessive thirst and hunger	Less than 20 percent of the iron in food is actually absorbed through the intestinal wall. The most common nutritional deficiency in the United States.

MINERAL	FUNCTION	GOOD SOURCES
Zinc	Wound healing; growth, skin structure; component of some enzymes and of the hormone insulin; immune system; brain neurotransmitters	Shellfish, meat, canned fish, hard cheese, whole grains, nuts, eggs
Copper	Used in forming the connective tissue of blood vessels; a component of some enzymes; used in forming bone and red blood cells; antioxidant; immune system functions	Shellfish, olives, nuts, beans and peas, whole-grain cereals, chocolate
Molybdenum	Starts enzymes working; normal sexual functioning in men	Dairy products, cereals, beans, bread, liver
Selenium	Used in the synthesis of an antioxidant enzyme that attacks cancer-causing substances; maintains liver functions	Meats, fish, whole grains, dairy products, cabbage, celery, broccoli, mushrooms
Iodine	Formation of thyroid hormones (regulators of body's rate of energy use)	Seafood, dairy products, drinking water (varies with local soils), onions
Chromium	Works with insulin to help cells get and use blood sugar	Liver, egg yolks, pepper, thyme, beef, poultry, broccoli, whole-grain cereals, bran
Fluorine (in the form of fluoride)	Stabilizes calcium in bones and teeth	Tea, coffee, meat, fish, cereal, fruit

SYMPTOMS OF DEFICIENCY	SYMPTOMS OF EXCESS	NOTES
Slow growth; delayed sexual maturity; loss of sense of taste; eczema; hair loss; apathy; sexual difficulties	Interference with copper metabolism; suppression of immune function; decreased levels of HDL cholesterol	Most zinc in foods is not absorbed.
Anemia; water retention; weakness of blood vessel walls; irritability; brittle bones; loss of sense of taste	Rare; nausea; vomiting; diarrhea; muscle pain; abnormal mental states; immune suppression	High levels of copper in the water may increase the rate of gastrointestinal upsets.
Rare occurrence in inherited diseases and those on long-term intravenous feeding	Weight loss; slow growth; anemia; diarrhea; swelling of joints; increased uric acid in blood	Molybdenum content of foods depends on the soils in which they were grown.
Occurs only in people living on foods grown in selenium-deficient soil.	Loss of hair and nails; skin inflammation; abnormal nerve functions; fatigue; irritability; dry hair	Some studies suggest selenium may combat depression.
Enlargement of the thyroid gland (goiter); a form of mental impairment called cretinism; hypothyroidism; deafness; abnormal fetal growth and brain development	Rare; may reduce thyroid hormone secretion; acne; inflammation of the salivary glands	Iodine is added to salt in the U.S. and several other countries.
High blood fat and cholesterol levels; diabetes-like symptoms	Irregular heartbeat	Chromium damages cells grown in laboratory cultures. Carcinogenic effects not confirmed in humans.
Bone thinning; risk of cavities in the teeth; osteoporosis	Bony outgrowths of the spine; mottling and pitting of the teeth; dermatitis; loss of appetite	Fluoridation of local water supplies reduces the rate of dental caries.

Table 3
SOME NUTRITIONAL DEFICIENCY DISEASES

DEFICIENT FACTOR	DISEASE	CAUSE
Calories (energy) and protein	Marasmus	General malnutrition: cells starved of both energy and building materials
Protein	Kwashiorkor	Body lacking amino acids needed for growth and repair
Vitamin A	Night blindness; xeropthalmia	The color-vision pigment in the eye requires vitamin A.
Thiamin	Beriberi	An enzyme of glucose metabolism cannot function without thiamin. Toxic wastes accumulate.
Thiamin	Wernicke's encephalopathy	An enzyme of glucose metabolism cannot function without thiamin. Toxic wastes accumulate.
Niacin	Pellagra	Many functions are disrupted.
B_{12} (cyanocobalamin)	Pernicious anemia	Folic acid and B_{12} are needed to form DNA. Without them, cells cannot divide.
Vitamin C	Scurvy	Vitamin C is needed to build collagen in skin and muscles.
Vitamin D	Rickets (in children); Osteomalacia (in adults)	Vitamin D is needed to promote calcium absorption from food.
Vitamin K	Hemorrhagic (bleeding) diseases	Vitamin K is needed to form blood-clotting factors in the liver.

SYMPTOMS	OCCURRENCE	NOTES
Underweight; loss of fat under skin; gastroenteritis; poor appetite; infections	Occurs in underfed children, especially in developing nations	
Skin discoloration and peeling; loss of appetite; apathy; swollen abdomen; blood abnormalities	Occurs in underfed children, especially in developing nations	
Loss of dim vision and (eventually) total blindness; hardening and drying of skin; respiratory infections; kidney stones	Highest in Bangladesh, India, Indonesia, and the Philippines; most often associated with protein malnutrition in children	Treated with high doses of vitamin A. The World Health Organization has made prevention of xeropthalmia a priority.
Small blood vessels dilate; heart failure	Now rare, although once common among rice-eating populations in East Asia; seen in some alcoholics	Treated over a period of weeks with a mix of B vitamins.
Brain malfunctions seen as confusion; memory loss; movement disorders	Alcoholics	Responds to treatment with B vitamins, but memory disorder may linger after treatment.
Thickening and cracking of the skin; diarrhea; mental confusion	Egypt and southern Africa where most of the diet is corn (tryptophan and niacin-deficient); also occurs in alcoholics.	Treated over a period of weeks with a mix of B vitamins. The vitamins can convert the amino-acid tryptophan to niacin.
Indigestion; diarrhea; waxy pallor; numbness; tingling of toes	Vegetarians; older people of northern European descent	Cells in bone marrow that should form red cells enlarge. Their nuclei are abnormal.
Swelling and bleeding of gums and skin; bleeding into the muscles and around the bones	Extremely rare today. Totally preventable with plant foods such as oranges, lemons, tomatoes, etc.	Historically, a prevalent disease among sailors who went for months without fruits and vegetables.
(In children): soft skull, bony nodules, bent bones; (in adults): bone cracks, brittle bones, pain and tenderness	Rare in sunny climates where sunshine stimulates vitamin D formation under the skin. Sometimes found among infants receiving only breast milk, institutionalized people, and the housebound elderly.	The addition of vitamin D to milk has made rickets uncommon. Dark skin is less efficient making vitamin D in sunlight than fair skin.
Excessive bleeding from wounds and internally	May be caused by disorders of fat absorption or brought on by drug treatment with certain antibiotics of anti-clotting drugs.	Treated with injections of vitamin K.

Table 4

SOME POPULAR HERBAL SUPPLEMENTS: CLAIMS, SIDE EFFECTS, AND CAUTIONS

HERB	CLAIM[1]	SIDE EFFECTS	NOTES
Echinacea	Speeds recovery from colds and flu, but does not prevent them	Diarrhea; heartburn; intestinal upsets; liver problems; skin rashes	Some preparations are contaminated with other plant species or bacteria. Do not use with drugs that affect liver or if allergic to ragweed. Because it suppresses immune system with long-term use, AIDS patients should not take it.
Ephedra (Ma huang)	Stimulates activity; controls weight; boosts energy; relieves asthma	Warning: Highly toxic! A relative of amphetamines and may be addictive. Increases blood pressure, heart rate. May cause palpitations, seizures, nervousness, headaches, insomnia, dizziness, and death.	Should be used only under the supervision of a physician.
Feverfew	Prevents and relieves migraine headaches	Nervousness; insomnia; fatigue; mouth ulcers; headaches; flatulence; slow blood clotting	Avoid prior to surgery. Do not take if pregnant, nursing, or allergic to ragweed.
Ginger	Relieves seasickness and motion sickness	Heartburn; allergies	Do not use for morning sickness or if you have gallbladder problems or take blood-thinning drugs.
Gingko biloba	Improves memory; mental acuity; and circulation of blood	Headaches; indigestion; nausea; rash; dizziness; bleeding	Reduces the ability of the blood to clot after injury or surgery. Avoid if allergic to cashews, mangoes, or poison ivy.
Ginseng	Boosts energy; improves sexual performance; counteracts stress and aging	Rapid heartbeat and high blood pressure; headaches; irregular menstrual periods; breast tenderness; insomnia	Should not be taken with stimulants, decongestants, blood thinners, or diabetic drugs. A rash may indicate a life-threatening allergic response. See a doctor immediately.
Kava	Reduces anxiety; promotes relaxation	Stomach and intestinal problems, liver disorders; allergic skin reactions; yellowing of skin and nails	Do not use with barbiturates, alcohol, or other depressants. Should not be used long-term without a doctor's supervision.
St. John's Wort	Elevates mood, relieves depression	Dizziness; dry mouth; fatigue; digestive problems; increased sensitivity to sunlight	Reduces the effectiveness of prescription drugs (antidepressants, birth-control pills, antibiotics, heart medicines, and others).

[1] Most claims are untested and unverified. The Food and Drug Administration does not regulate herbs sold as food supplements. This table is not intended for use as a diagnostic or treatment tool. Check with your physician before using any herbal supplements.

NOTES

Foreword

1. Estimate from the Enzyme Commission.

Chapter One

1. Personal communication, Dr. Marion Stankovich, Chemist, University of Minnesota.
2. V. R. Young and A. E. El-Khoury, "Human Amino Acid Requirements: A Re-Evaluation," *The United Nations University Press: Food and Nutrition Bulletin* (September 1996).
3. N. Moller and K. S. Nair. "Regulation of Muscle Mass and Function: Effects of Aging and Hormones," in *The Role of Protein and Amino Acids in Sustaining and Enhancing Performance* (Washington, D.C.: National Academy Press, 1999), p. 121.
4. American Medical Association, Charles B. Clayman, (Editor). *A Healthy Digestion.* Pleasantville, NY: Reader's Digest Association, 1992, p. 32.
5. J. Doedtman, "The Protein Question," at http://www.sobefit.com/resources/articles/nat4.htm.
6. "Endocrine Tumors of the Pancreas," at http://www.endocrineweb.com/pancreas.html.
7. G. Noyes-Hull, "The Good, the Bad, and the Nasty," *Odyssey* (October 2000), pp. 19–20.
8. William Ganong, *Review of Medical Physiology,* 19th ed. (Stamford, CT: Appleton and Lange, 1999).
9. Data from the USDA Nutrient Analysis Laboratory. [Iceberg lettuce at 12 kcal per 100 grams. Hershey's Special Dark, Sweet Chocolate (2.2 oz. bar) at 342 kcal.]

10. H. C. Slavkin, "Toward 'Molecular Gastronomy,' or What's in a Taste?" National Institute of Dental and Craniofacial Research: *Insights on Human Health* (October 1999).

11. Bernard Lyman, *The Psychology of Taste* (New York: Van Nostrand, 1989), p. 139.

12. M. H. K. Fisher, *The Gastronomical Me*. In *The Art of Eating* (New York: Random House, 1976), p. 353.

13. Data from the National Center for Health Statistics, 1997.

14. A. A. Butler, R. A. Ketserson, K. Khong, M. J. Cullen, M. A. Pelleymounter, J. Dekoining, M. Baetscher, and R. D. Cone, "A Unique Syndrome Causes Obesity in the Melanin-3 Receptor-deficient Mouse." *Endocrinology* (September 14, 2000): pp. 3518–3521.

15. Raloff, Janet, "Is Obesity Contagious?" *Science News Online* (April 12, 1997).

16. Ibid.

17. N. V. Dhurandhar, B. A. Israel, J. M. Kolesar, G.F. Mayhew, M.E. Cook, and R. L. Atkinson, "Increased Adiposity in Animals Due to a Human Virus," *International Journal of Obesity* (August 2000), pp. 989–996.

Chapter Two

1. "Odyssey Asks a Brain Scientist," *Odyssey* (October 2000), p. 26.

2. Alpha-Tocopherol, Beta Carotene Cancer Prevention Study Group. "The Effect of Vitamin E and Beta Carotene on the Incidence of Lung Cancer and Other Cancers in Male Smokers," *New England Journal of Medicine* 330 (1994): 1029–1035.

3. Yokoyama, Tetsuji and others, "Serum Vitamin C Concentration Was Inversely Associated with Subsequent 20-year Incidence of Stroke in a Japanese Rural Community: The Shibata Study," *Stroke 2000* 31: 2287–2294.

4. A. Ascherio, E. Rimm, M. Hernán, E. Giovannucci, I. Kawachi, M. Stampfer, and W. Willett, "Relation of Consumption of Vitamin E, Vitamin C, and Carotenoids to Risk for Stroke Among Men in the United States." *Annals of Internal Medicine* (June 15, 1999), pp. 963–970.

5. Op. cit., *Odyssey*.

6. "Cholesterol: Knowledge Behind Your Numbers," *Mayo Clinic Health Letter* (June 1993: updated by *Health Oasis*, Mayo Clinic, September 24, 1998).

7. Jeanine Barone, "Which Foods Affect Cholesterol?" February 6, 1999 at http://onhealth.com/ch1/in-depth/item/item,37237_1_1.asp.

8. Graham A. Colditz, "Prudent Diet," for www.medscape.com.

9. Nutritional data from McDonald's Nutrition chart and a menu of traditional Thanksgiving recipes and nutritional analyses available from www.cooking.com.

10. Public Information Committee for the American Society for Nutritional Sciences and the American Society for Clinical Nutrition, "One-Third of the American Diet Is Junk Food; The Other Two-Thirds Don't Achieve 100% of the Recommended Daily Allowance." Press release, September 25, 2000.

11. Judy McBride, "Added-Sugar Intake on the Rise," *Agricultural Research* (June 2000).

12. Ibid.

13. Nicole M. de Roos, Michiel L. Bots, and Martijn B. Katan, "Replacement of Dietary Saturated Fatty Acids by Trans Fatty Acids Lowers Serum HDL Cholesterol and Impairs Endothelial Function in Healthy Men and Women," *Arteriosclerosis, Thrombosis and Vascular Biology* 21: 1233–1237.

14. American Medical Association, Charles B. Clayman (Editor). *A Healthy Digestion*. Pleasantville, NY: Reader's Digest Association, 1992, p. 25.

15. Second edition (New York: Owl Books, 1999).

16. Data from the National Osteoporosis Foundation.

17. Dawson-Hughes, Bess. "Osteoporosis: A Call to Action," Medical Education Collaborative 2000 at http://www.medscape.com.

18. "Osteoporosis in Men: Bone Up on the Facts," Mayo Foundation for Medical Education and Research, February 21, 2001, at http://www.mayoclinic.com.

19. American Academy of Orthopaedic Surgeons, "Weight-bearing Exercise Reduces Osteoporosis Risk," (July 5, 2000).

20. "Fill Your Plate—and Fight Cancer," *Woman's Day* (February 1, 2001), p. 43.

21. Graham Colditz, "Prudent Diet," for medscape.com.

22. Harvey Weingarten, "Food Cravings in a College Population," *Appetite* (1991), pp. 167–175.

23. Colleen Pierre, "Conquer Your Cravings," *American Health* (April 1999), p. 92.

24. "Maryland Students Prove Eating School Breakfast Improves Academic Performance," American School Food Service Association, March 9, 2000.

25. International Food Information Council, "Breakfast: Waking Up to a Healthy Start" at http://ificinfo.health.org/insight/breakfst.htm.

26. "Breakfast Is Important for Your Children—Advice from ADA," *American Dietetics Association News Update* (August 2000).

27. A. K. Kant, A. Schatzkin, B. Graubard, and C. Schairer, "A Prospective Study of Diet Quality and Mortality in Women," *Journal of the American Medical Association* (April 26, 2000), pp. 2109–2115.

28. Priscilla Hollander, "Successful Weight Management Tools and Practices," In *Medscape Diabetes and Endocrinology Treatment Updates: Multiple Risk Factors in Diabetes: Focus on Obesity* at www.medscape.com.

29. P. M. Kris-Etherton, T. A. Pearson, Y. Wan, R. L. Hargrove, K. Moriarty, V. Fishell, and T. Etherton. "High Mono-Unsaturated Fatty Acid Diets Lower Plasma Cholesterol and Triacylglycerol Concentrations," *American Journal of Clinical Nutrition* (December 1999), pp. 1009–1015.

30. Priscilla Hollander, "Successful Weight Management Tools and Practices," in *Medscape Diabetes and Endocrinology Treatment Updates: Multiple Risk Factors in Diabetes: Focus on Obesity* at www.medscape.com.

31. "Obesity Has Reached Epidemic Proportions," Press Release from the American College of Nutrition, October 5, 2000.

Chapter Three

1. I. L. Pike, "The Nutritional Consequences of Pregnancy Sickness: A Critique of a Hypothesis," *Human Nature* (2000) 11:3, p. 207.

2. Gordon Conway, "Food for All in the 21st Century," *Social Research* (Spring 1999).

3. Estimate from the charitable organization "America's Second Harvest."

4. Data from the National Center for Health Statistics, 1997.

5. "Pullout Vitamin Chart: Take the Perfect Vitamins," *Prevention*, January 2001.

6. Lisa Miller, "Heartburn." *Woman's Day* (December 12, 2000), p. 42.

7. Press release from the University of Maryland Medical Center, "Quarterback Dedicates Championship to Daughter with Celiac Disease," January 1, 2001.

8. Data from the American Diabetes Association.

9. Ibid.

10. Janet Raloff, "The New GI Tracks," *Science News* (April 8, 2000).

11. Loraine Stern, "Your Child's Health: Type 2 Diabetes," *Woman's Day* (November 1, 2000), p. 146.

12. "Nutritional Medicine Latest Weapon in War Against Type 2 Diabetes," Press Release from ScienceBased Health (November 21, 2000).

13. Dianne Hales, "Should You Be Checked for Diabetes?" *Parade Magazine* (February 4, 2001), p. 4.

14. Jerry Adler and Claudia Kalb, "An American Epidemic: Diabetes," *Newsweek* (September 4, 2000), p. 42.

15. "Nutritional Medicine Latest Weapon in War Against Type 2 Diabetes," Press Release from ScienceBased Health (November 21, 2000).

16. C. M. Steppan, S. Bailey, S. Bhat, E. Brown, R. Banerjee, C. Wright, H. Paxtel, R. Ahima, and M. Lazarr. "The Hormone Resistin Links Obesity to Diabetes," *Nature* (January 18, 2001), pp. 307–312.

17. John Miles, "Insulin Resistance Syndrome," in "Multiple Risk Factors in Diabetes: Focus on Obesity," Medical Education Collaborative: 2001, at www.medscape.com.

18. "Diabetes Medical Essay: Prevention and Treatment," *Health Oasis* (April 14, 2000).
19. Morris Birnbaum, "Dialogue Between Muscle and Fat," *Nature* (February 8, 2001), pp. 672–673.
20. J. Salmeron, A. Ascherio, E. B. Rimm, and others. "Dietary Fiber, Glycemic Load, and the Risk of NIDDM in Men," *Diabetes Care* 1997 (20): 545
21. "Exercise May Be 'Best Drug' for Insulin Resistance Syndrome," A report from the 56th annual meeting of the American Diabetes Association (June 8, 1996).
22. Ibid.
23. According to the International Pancreas Transplant Registry at the University of Minnesota, 2001.
24. American Diabetes Association, "Stem Cell Research," at http://www.diabetes.org.
25. A. T. Cheung, B. Dayanandan, J. T. Lewis, G. S. Korbutt, R. V. Rajotte, M. Bryer-Ash, M. O. Boylan, M. M. Wolfe, T. J. Kieffer. "Glucose-Dependent Insulin Release from Genetically Engineered K Cells," *Science 2000*; 290 (5498): 1959–1962.
26. Marvin M. Schuster, M. D. Crowell, and N. J. Talley. "Irritable Bowel Syndrome (IBS): Examining New Findings and Treatments," (October 26, 2000) Promeda: 2000 (on Medscape); "Irritable Bowel Syndrome Under-diagnosed," Press release from the American College of Gastroenterology, October 12, 2000.
27. "Irritable Bowel Syndrome, Intestinal Bacteria May Be Linked," Press release from Cedars-Sinai Medical Center, December 14, 2000.
28. American Medical Association, Charles B. Clayman (Editor). *A Healthy Digestion*. Pleasantville, NY: Reader's Digest Association, 1992, p. 11.
29. All data in this section from the American Cancer Society, except as separately noted.
30. Estimate from the University of Chicago Hospitals and Health System.
31. Alexander Rosemurgy and Francesco Serafini, "New Directions in Systematic Therapy of Pancreatic Cancer," Moffitt Cancer Center and Research Institute: *Cancer Control*, 2000.
32. "Folate and Colorectal Cancer: A Consistent Story," Press release from the American College of Nutrition, October 5, 2000.
33. Susan Rainey, "Rooting Out a Major Killer," *Newsweek* (July 31, 2000), p. 59.
34. K. Halmi, S. Sunday, M. Strober, A. Kaplan, D. Woodside, M. Fichter, J. Tresure, W. Berrettini, and W. Kaye, "Perfectionism in Anorexia Nervosa: Variation by Clinical Subtype, Obesessionality, and Pathological Eating Behavior," *American Journal of Psychiatry* (November 2000): 1799–1805.
35. C. M. Bulik, P. F. Sullivan, T. D. Wade, and K. S. Kendler, "Twin Studies on Eating Disorders: A Review," *International Journal of Eating Disorders* (2000) 27:1–20.

36. Lisa Jennifer Selzman, "Eating Disorders: Born or Made," *American Health* (October 1999), p. 53.
37. Data from Support Concern and Resources for Eating Disorders, 2000.
38. Estimate from the American Anorexia/Bulimia Association, Inc.
39. "Binge Eating and Substance Abuse Among Adolescents," *Nutrition Research Newsletter* (November 1999).
40. Connor, Steve, "Most Animals Have Prions, Proteins That Can Cause Fatal Nervous Diseases. So Why Do We Have Them in the First Place?" *The Independent* (London) (November 12, 1999).
41. Debora MacKenzie, "This Week: BSE Report: How It Went Horribly Wrong," *New Scientist* (November 4, 2000): 4–9.
42. Estimate from the Creutzfeldt-Jakob Disease Foundation.
43. P. Brown, R. Will, R. Bradley, D. Asher, and L. Detwiler, "Bovine-Spongiform Encephalopathy and Variant Creutzfeldt-Jakob Disease: Background, Evolution, and Current Concerns," CDC: *Emerging Infectious Diseases* (January–February 2001).
44. Some scientists think BSE may have arisen as a spontaneous mutation in British cattle, rather than being transferred from sheep. In either case, the assertion that BSE produced CJD is not questioned. See Paul Brown, "Bovine Spongiform Encephalopathy and Variant Creutzfeldt-Jakob Disease," *British Medical Journal* 322 (April 7, 2001): 841–844.
45. Brown and others, op cit.
46. Ibid.
47. Ibid.

Chapter Four

1. Kathiann Kowalski, "Faking It in the World of Fats and Sugars," *Odyssey* (October 2000): 36–37.
2. "Congress Gives Saccharin a Clean 'Bill' of Health: Warning Label to be Removed," December 22, 2000, PRNewswire.
3. "Saccharin Should Not Have Been Delisted," May 12, 2000, Center for Science in the Public Interest.
4. Paul Barton, "FDA Asked to Change Warning on Olestra," *The Seattle Times* (June 16, 1998).
5. U.S. Air Force Pamphlet on the Medical Defense against Biological Material.
6. U.S. Food and Drug Administration, "Keeping the Nation's Food Supply Safe: FDA's Big Job Done Well," Publication No. FS 01-2, May 2001.
7. *Bad Bug Book, Foodborne Pathogenic Microorganisms and Natural Toxins Handbook,* U.S. Food and Drug Administration, Center for Food Safety and Applied Nutrition, Chapter 1, "*Salmonella* spp."

8. Ibid., Chapter 6, "*Listeria monocytogenes.*"
9. Ibid., Chapter 19, "*Shigella* spp."
10. Audrey Hingley, "*Campylobacter*: Low-Profile Bug Is Food Poisoning Leader," *FDA Consumer* (September–October 1999).
11. Op. cit., Chapter 4, "*Campylobacter jejuni.*"
12. N. A. Daniels and A. Shafaie, "A Review of Pathogenic Vibrio Infections for Clinicians," *Infections in Medicine* (October 2000): 665–685.
13. P. S. Mead, L. Slutsker, V. Dietz, L. F. McCaig, J. S. Bresee, C. Shapiro, P. M. Griffin, and R. V. Tauxe, "Food-Related Illness and Death in the United States," Centers for Disease Control: *Emerging Infectious Diseases* (September–October, 1999).
14. "Basic Biology of Cryptosporidium," Division of Biology, Parasitology Laboratory, Kansas State University, Updated December 7, 2000.
15. Op. cit., P. S. Mead, et al.
16. "Diarrhea: *E. coli:* Preventing a Common Type of Food Poisoning," at MayoClinic Online.
17. "*E. coli* Outbreak Strikes Wisconsin Schoolchildren," Reuters News Service, October 26, 2000.
18. "*Escherichia coli* O157:H7, Technical Information," Division of Bacterial and Mycotic Disease: Disease Information Centers for Disease Control and Prevention (December 2000).
19. L. Roberts, L. Jorm, M. Patel, W. Smith, R. M. Douglas, and C. Gilchrist. "Effect of Infection Control Measures on the Frequency of Diarrheal Episodes in Child Care: A Randomized, Controlled Trial," *Pediatrics* (April 2000), pp. 743–46.
20. "*Salmonella enteritidis* Infection," Division of Bacterial and Mycotic Diseases, Centers for Disease Control at http://www.cdc.gov/ncidod/publications/brochures/salmon.htm.
21. "Eggs to Carry Health Warning," Associated Press Online (November 30, 2000).
22. "Shellfish Increasing Harbingers of Dangerous Microbes," University of Arizona Press Release, December 1, 2000, at http://www.newswise.com.
23. R. R. Griffiths and Ellen M. Vernotica, "Is Caffeine a Flavoring Agent in Cola Soft Drinks?" *Archives of Family Medicine* (August 2000), p. 727.
24. Michael Jacobson, "Liquid Candy: How Soft Drinks Are Harming Americans' Health," Center for Science in the Public Interest.
25. Ibid.
26. Estimate from the Food Marketing Institute.
27. Charles E. Hanrahan, "The European Union's Ban on Hormone-Treated Meat," *Congressional Research Service Issue Brief for Congress*, National Council for Science and the Environment, December 19, 2000.

28. "The Use of Hormones for Growth Promotion in Food-Producing Animals," *Information for Consumers*, U.S. Food and Drug Administration, (May 1996).
29. Amanda Spake, "Natural Hazards," *U.S. News & World Report* (February 12, 2001), p. 43.
30. Faith Brynie, "'Prospecting' for Drugs" *Odyssey* (February 2000), p. 12.
31. Op cit., p. 49.
32. "Herbal R$_x$: The Promises and Pitfalls," *Consumer Reports* (March 1999), p. 45.
33. "NFPA Applauds Establishment of National Organic Standard, But Notes 'Organic' Does Not Mean Safer or More Nutritious," PR Newswire, December 21, 2000.
34. Sandra Gordon, "The Case for Organic Food," *New Age* (September/October 1999), p. 70.
35. P. Reaney, "Super-Broccoli Plants Bred to Prevent Cancer," Reuters News Service, May 24, 2000.
36. "Seeds of Change," *Consumer Reports* (Sep 1999), p. 41.
37. "Africa Needs Gene-Modified Crops," Reuters News Service, September 11, 2000.
38. "Seeds of Change" op. cit.
39. "Pica: Dirt Eating or 'Geophagy,'" from Support Concern and Resources for Eating Disorders (SCaRED).
40. Ellen Simpson, J. Dennis Mull, Erin Longley, and Joan East, "Pica during Pregnancy in Low-Income Women Born in Mexico," *Western Journal of Medicine* (July 2000), pp. 20–24.

Chapter Five

1. "Functional Foods—Position of ADA," *Journal of the American Dietetic Association* 99 (1999): 1278–1285. The quoted definition is attributed to the International Food Information Council.
2. The Institute of Medicine and the National Academy of Sciences limit the definition of functional foods to those in which the concentration of at least one ingredient has been modified to enhance the contribution of the food to a healthful diet.
3. C. E. Butterworth Jr., and A. Bendich, "Folic Acid and the Prevention of Birth Defects," *Annual Review of Nutrition* 16 (1996): 73–97.
4. Estimate from the Centers for Disease Control and Prevention, Atlanta.
5. Margaret A. Honein, Leonard J. Paulozzi, T. J. Mathews, J. David Erickson, and Lee-Yang C. Wong, "Impact of Folic Acid Fortification of the U.S. Food Supply on the Occurrence of Neural Tube Defects," *Journal of the American Medical Association* 285 (June 20, 2001): 2981–2986.

6. "Vitamin That Prevents Birth Defects," Press release from the March of Dimes Birth Defects Foundation, August 18, 2001.

7. M. A. Hallikainen and M. I. Uusitupa, "Effects of Two Low-Fat Stanol Ester-Containing Margarines on Serum Cholesterol Concentrations as Part of a Low-Fat Diet in Hypercholesterolemic Subjects," *American Journal of Clinical Nutrition* (1999), pp. 403–410.

8. "Margarines Can Benefit People with Mildly High Cholesterol," Reuters Health, September 11, 2000.

9. John W. Erdman for the AHA Nutrition Committee, "Soy Protein and Cardiovascular Health," *Circulation* (November 14, 2000), p. 2555.

10. John Henkl, "Soy: Health Claims for Soy Protein, Questions About Other Components," *FDA Consumer* (May–June 2000).

11. Third International Symposium on the Role of Soy in Preventing and Treating Chronic Disease, 1999.

12. "Chemicals in Broccoli Can Cut Lung Cancer Risk," Reuters News Service, September 22, 2000.

13. Stephanie J. London, Jian-Min Yuan, Fung-Lung Chung, Yu-Tang Gao, Gerhard A. Coetzee, Ronald K. Ross, Mimi C. Yu, "Isothiocyanates, Glutathione S-transferase M1 and T1 Polymorphisms, and Lung-Cancer Risk: A Prospective Study of Men in Shanghai, China," *Lancet* 356 (August 26, 2000): 724.

14. Elizabeth Somer, "Food and Mood," *American Health* (April 1995), p. 58.

15. Faith Brynie, "Can Milk Make You Happy? Can Fish Make You Smart?" *Odyssey* (October 2000), pp. 24–27.

16. Ibid.

17. Rachel Rabkin, "Medical News, " *Family Circle* (February 1, 2001), p. 58.

18. Nina Elder, "Herbs Can Hurt You During Surgery," *Better Homes and Gardens* (November 1999), p. 138.

19. "Odyssey Asks a Brain Scientist," *Odyssey* (October 2000), p. 26.

20. American Institute for Cancer Research, "The New American Plate," brochure.

21. David Spurgeon, "Researchers Find Conflicting Evidence on Benefits of Garlic," *British Medical Journal* (October 124, 2000), p. 918. See A. T. Fleischauer, C. Poole, and L. Arab, " Garlic Consumption and Cancer Prevention: Meta-analyses of Colorectal and Stomach Cancer," *American Journal of Clinical Nutrition* (October 2000), pp. 1047–1052.

22. "Garlic: Effects on Cardiovascular Risks and Disease, Protective Effects Against Cancer, and Clinical Adverse Effects," *Evidence Report/Technology Assessment: Number 20,* AHRQ Publication No. 01-E022, October 2000.

23. Faith Brynie. "The Plant Medicine Hall of Fame," *Odyssey* (February 2001): 10–13.

24. Steve Bunk, "Micronutrients and Infection: Vitamins and Minerals Are Proving to Be Effective Disease Battlers," *The Scientist* (April 17, 2000).
25. Data from the charitable organization America's Second Harvest.
26. "Biotechnology Could Solve Africa's Food Problems," Panafrican News Agency, November 13, 2000.
27. Claire Wallerstein, "New Sweet Potato Could Help Combat Blindness in Africa," *British Medical Journal* (September 30, 2000), p. 786.

GLOSSARY

Abdomen: the part of the body that contains the stomach, pancreas, intestines, liver, gallbladder, and other organs.

Active transport: a process by which cells use energy to move molecules through membranes.

Amino acids: the building block molecules from which proteins are made.

Anemia: an insufficiency of the oxygen-carrying molecule hemoglobin or in the number of red blood cells or a depleted total volume of blood.

Anorexia nervosa: an eating disorder characterized by self-starvation.

Antioxidant: any of a number of substances including plant hormones and certain vitamins and minerals that prevent free radicals (charged molecules) from combining with oxygen and (as a result) inflicting damage on artery walls.

Appendix: a small, wormlike extension of the colon that lies near its juncture with the small intestine.

Artificial selection: see *Selective breeding.*

ATP (adenosine triphosphate): the body's main energy-transfer compound.

Bile: a product made by the liver and stored in the gallbladder. It breaks down fats in the duodenum.

BSE (bovine spongiform encephalopathy): a disease of cattle characterized by degeneration of the brain and nervous system. Also called "mad cow disease."

Bulimia: an eating disorder characterized by binge eating and purging, either by vomiting or with laxatives.

Calorie: see *Kilocalorie.*

Cancer: any of many diseases characterized by cell division out of control. Specific forms are named for the organ in which they originate.

Capillaries: tiny blood vessels through which materials are exchanged between cells and the bloodstream.

Carbohydrate: a category of chemicals that includes compounds made of carbon, hydrogen, and oxygen. A major category of food.

Carbon-based: designating any molecule in which the primary structure is made of carbon atoms.

Celiac disease (or celiac sprue): an inherited intolerance to the protein gluten found in wheat and other grains.

Cellulose: an indigestible carbohydrate found in the cell walls of plants.

Chemotherapy: treatment with anticancer drugs.

Cholesterol: a fatlike substance produced in the liver and plentiful in fatty foods from animal sources (such as meat, whole milk, and egg yolks).

CJD (Creutzfeldt-Jakob Disease): a degenerative disease of the nervous system and brain in humans.

Collagen: a protein found in muscle, tendons, and skin.

Colon: large intestine.

Colonoscopy: the examination of the inside of the colon using a thin, lighted tube inserted through the rectum.

Colorectal: having to do with the colon or rectum.

Crohn's disease: see *Inflammatory bowel disease.*

Crossbreeding: the use of closely related species as parents to produce a new strain of organism.

Diabetes: a disease caused by the production of too little insulin in the pancreas or by the resistance of body cells to the action of insulin.

Diffuse: to travel and mix gradually due to random movement of molecules.

Digestion: the breakdown of large food molecules into smaller ones.

DNA (deoxyribonucleic acid): the basic material of inheritance found in the nucleus of many cells.

Dopamine: a neurotransmitter that causes glands to produce hormones, regulates movement, and plays a part in emotions and learning.

Duodenum: the upper part of the small intestine, where most digestion occurs.

Energy density: the caloric value of food per unit of weight or volume.

Enzyme: a protein that speeds up biochemical reactions in cells.

Epiglottis: a muscular flap at the back of the mouth that closes over the windpipe during swallowing.

Epinephrine: a hormone secreted by the adrenal gland in response to stress. It increases blood pressure and heart rate, preparing the body for action.

Esophagus: the food tube that connects the mouth and stomach.

Fat: a general term for chemicals that are made of fatty acids and glycerol. A category of energy-rich foods that includes butter, margarine, and vegetable oils.

FDA: the U. S. Food and Drug Administration, an agency that oversees food testing, quality, labeling, and more.

Fiber: large, stable carbohydrate molecules in plant foods that humans can't digest.

Free radical: a charged molecule that can damage body cells when combined with oxygen.

Functional foods (also called designer foods or nutraceuticals): foods said to provide health benefits beyond basic nutrition.

Galanin: a hormone made by the hypothalamus in the brain that increases appetite and decreases energy use.

Gallbladder: the organ that stores bile.

Gastrin: a hormone made and released by the stomach that stimulates both stomach action and secretion of enzymes from the pancreas.

Gastrocolic reflex: contractions of the intestine triggered by ingestion of food.

Genetic modification (also called genetic engineering, transgenic engineering, genetic alteration, gene technology, biotechnology, and recombinant DNA technology): the transfer of genes from one species to another.

Glucose: the simple sugar the body uses for energy.

Glycogen: a carbohydrate produced by the liver that stores energy in the body.

GRAS (Generally Recognized as Safe): a classification concerning food additives.

Heartburn: a burning feeling in the chest resulting from the backup of stomach acid into the esophagus.

Heart disease: a condition involving the blockage of the arteries that supply the heart muscle.

Hemoglobin: the iron-containing pigment in the red blood cells of humans and some other animals that carries oxygen and makes blood red.

High-density lipoprotein (HDL): the "good" cholesterol; a molecule that removes cholesterol from the bloodstream by carrying it to the liver for disposal.

Hormone: a chemical made by one organ that travels through the bloodstream and affects another organ.

Hydrolysis: the splitting of a large molecule by inserting a water molecule into it.

Hypothalamus: a gland in the brain involved in regulating body functions and temperature, hunger, and thirst, and in secreting hormones that affect the body's "master gland," the pituitary.

Immune system: the white blood cells, enzymes, antibodies, and other mechanisms that defend the body against disease.

Immunotherapy: the use of the body's own immune defenses to destroy cancer cells.

Inflammation: the swelling, redness, pain, heat, and stiffness of an infection or injury resulting from actions of the immune system.

Inflammatory bowel disease: a disorder characterized by chronic inflammation (immune system attack) of the lining of the intestines.

Insulin: the hormone made by the pancreas that regulates the movement of glucose molecules from the bloodstream into body cells.

Ion: a charged atom or small molecule.

Irritable bowel syndrome: intestinal pain and gas caused by strong, frequent contractions of the intestine after a meal.

Kilocalorie (also calorie): in the English system of measurement in use in the United States, the unit used to express the amount of energy in food.

"Knockout": designating experimental animals, usually mice, bred for research purposes to lack a particular gene (the "knocked-out" gene).

Leptin: a hormone made by fat cells that curbs appetite.

Lipase: a fat-digesting enzyme.

Liver: the reddish brown organ in the upper right abdomen that filters blood, secretes bile, stores glucose as glycogen, detoxifies drugs and poisons, and performs many other vital functions.

Low-density lipoprotein (LDL): the "bad" cholesterol; the carrier of cholesterol that contributes to the formation of plaque in artery walls.

Lymph: the clear fluid that surrounds body cells and carries the defensive cells of the immune system.

Membrane: a thin outer covering, such as that surrounding a cell or its nucleus.

Metabolism: the chemical reactions that fuel and maintain the body.

Micelle: a sphere of molecules that moves fat from the intestine into the bloodstream.

Microvilli: see *Villi.*

Mineral: an inorganic (noncarbon) substance or element required by the living body.

Mitochondria: the structures in cells where energy is released from food.

Monounsaturated fat: a slightly unsaturated fat found in olives, peanuts, avocados, and canola oil. See also *Unsaturated fat* and *Polyunsaturated fat.*

Neurotransmitter: a substance that carries a nerve impulse from one nerve cell to another.

NPY (neuropeptide Y): a hormone made by the hypothalamus that increases feeding behavior.

Organelle: a specialized structure within a cell.

Organic: in chemistry, carbon-based. In the food industry, foods grown free of synthetic pesticides or chemical fertilizers.

Osteoporosis: a disease characterized by brittle bones that break easily.

Parasite: an organism that maintains its own life at the expense of another organism, its host.

Pathogen: an organism that causes disease.

Pepsin: an enzyme in the stomach that breaks proteins into amino acids.

Peptide: a short chains of amino acids.

Pica: the abnormal craving for substances or objects that are not foods.

Pituitary gland: a gland that secretes many hormones that affect other organs and systems.

Polyunsaturated fat: a highly unsaturated fat found in safflower, sunflower, corn, and soybean oil. See also *Unsaturated fat* and *Monounsaturated fat.*

Prion: a protein found in cells that, when abnormally shaped, causes disease such as BSE and CJD.

Protein: any of a class of chemicals composed of amino acids; a major food group, which includes meats, eggs, peanut butter, and soybeans.

Radiation therapy: the use of high-energy rays or particles to kill cancer cells.

Receptor: a site on the surface of a cell membrane that binds a particular molecule, much as a lock accepts a key.

Risk factor: any influence that increases the chance of a developing a disease.

RNA: The genetic material (as opposed to DNA) of some viruses; in DNA-containing cells, RNA acts as a messenger, carrying the protein-making instructions of DNA (in the nucleus) to the ribosomes (in the cytoplasm) where proteins are made.

Saturated fats: fats that are solid at room temperature, including animal fats, butter, and vegetable fats that have been treated with hydrogen to make them hard (as in some margarines).

Selective breeding: the manipulation of characteristics in a species achieved by selecting the parents and breeding them for a desired trait.

Serotonin: a neurotransmitter that influences mood, sleeping, and waking.

Sigmoidoscopy: inspection of the lower colon, using a thin, lighted tube to collect samples of cells for examination under a microscope.

Stress: mental or physical tension brought on by emotional factors or physical overexertion.

Stroke: loss of some part of brain function resulting from the blockage of blood supply to brain tissue.

Triglyceride: a molecule made of three fatty acids attached to one glycerol molecule.

Trypsin: a protein-digesting enzyme.

TSH (thyroid-stimulating hormone, or thyrotropin): a hormone made by the pituitary gland that stimulates the thyroid gland to release still other hormones.

Ulcer: a sore in the stomach or intestine that does not heal.

Ulcerative colitis: see *Inflammatory bowel disease.*

Unsaturated fat: a fat that is usually liquid at room temperature and does not have hydrogen atoms (either naturally present or added) that make it hard. See also *Monounsaturated fat* and *Polyunsaturated fat.*

Villi (singular, villus): tiny, finger-shaped projections in the wall of the small intestine through which food molecules pass from the digestive system into the bloodstream.

Vitamin: an organic substance necessary to body chemistry but not used as an energy source.

White blood cells: cells in the blood of several different types, which fight disease and provide immunity.

FOR FURTHER INFORMATION

BOOKS

American Medical Association. *A Healthy Digestion*. Charles B. Clayman (Editor). Pleasantville, NY: Reader's Digest Association, 1992.

Arnold, Nick. *Disgusting Digestion* (Horrible Science Series). New York: Scholastic, 1999.

Avraham, Regina. *The Digestive System*. Broomall, PA: Chelsea House, 2000.

Bliss, Michael. *The Discovery of Insulin*. Chicago: University of Chicago Press, 1984.

Chevallier, Andrew. *The Encyclopedia of Medicinal Plants*. New York: Dorling Kindersley, 1996.

Costin, Carolyn. *The Eating Disorder Sourcebook: A Comprehensive Guide to the Causes, Treatments, and Prevention of Eating Disorders*. Rancho Santa Fe, CA: Lowell, 1999.

Graedon, Joe and Teresa Graedon. *The People's Pharmacy Guide to Home and Herbal Remedies*. New York: St. Martin's Press, 1999.

Institute for Food and Development Policy. *The Paradox of Plenty: Hunger in a Bountiful World*. Oakland, CA: Food First Books, 1999.

Krizmanic, Judy. *A Teen's Guide to Going Vegetarian*. New York: Puffin, 1994.

Levenkron, Steven. *Anatomy of Anorexia*. New York: Norton, 2000.

Pierson, Stephanie. *Vegetables Rock! A Complete Guide for Teenage Vegetarians*. New York: Bantam Doubleday Dell, 1999.

Pond, Caroline M. *The Fats of Life*. Cambridge, UK: Cambridge University Press, 1998.

Reavley, Nicola. *The New Encyclopedia of Vitamins, Minerals, Supplements, and Herbs*. New York: M. Evans, 1999.

Rinzler, Carol Ann, *Nutrition for Dummies*. New York: Hungry Minds, 1999.

Stanley, Debbie. *Understanding Bulimia Nervosa* (Teen Eating Disorder Prevention Book). New York: Rosen, 1999.

Vesanto, Melina, Brenda Davis, and Victoria Harrison. *Becoming Vegetarian: The Complete Guide to Adopting a Healthy Vegetarian Diet*. Summertown, TN: The Book Publishing Company, 1995.

Zampieron, Eugene R., and Ellen Kamhi. *The Natural Medicine Chest*. New York: Evans, 1999.

ON THE INTERNET

Australian Vegetarian Society Web site: www.moreinfo.com.au/avs/

Articles from the *FDA Consumer* magazine at http://www.fda.gov/opacom.catalog

Search for the nutrient values of foods through the Nutrient Analysis Laboratory of the U.S. Department of Agriculture at http:///www.nal.usda.gov/fnic/

Cutting-edge research on genetic modification of crop plants at Cornell University's Boyce Thompson Institute for Plant Research: www.birch.cit.cornell.edu

Stills and videos for normal and diseased parts of the digestive system at http://gastrointestinalatlas.com

The Natural Pharmacist at www.tnp.com

The National Institutes of Health Office of Dietary Supplements at www.nal.usda.gov/fnic/IBIDS

Natural Medicines Comprehensive Database at www.naturaldatabase.com

Mayo Health Clinic Oasis Web site: www.mayohealth.org

Plant-breeding techniques at the Vegetable Improvement Center at www.vic.tamu.edu

American Institute for Cancer Research, The New American Plate (booklet) at www.aicr.org/NAPbook.htm

University of Maryland Center for Celiac Research at www.celiaccenter.org

For in-depth information on a variety of foodborne pathogens, parasites, viruses, and toxins, see the FDA's *Bad Bug Book* at http://vm.cfsan.fda.gov/~mow/intro.html.

AGENCIES AND ORGANIZATIONS

American Anorexia/Bulimia Association
165 W. 46th Street, Suite 108
New York, NY 10036
Publishes a newsletter three times a year.
www.aabainc.org

American Cancer Society
1599 Clifton Road NE
Atlanta, GA 30309
Publishes information on all kinds of cancers, prevention, and treatment.
www.cancer.org

American Diabetes Association
1701 North Beauregard Street
Alexandria, VA 22311
Publishes the *American Diabetes Association Complete Guide to Diabetes.*
www.diabetes.org

American Dietetic Association
216 W. Jackson Boulevard, Suite 800
Chicago, IL 60606
Publishes the *American Dietetic Association's Complete Food and Nutrition Guide.*
www.eatright.org

American Heart Association National Center
7272 Greenville Avenue
Dallas, TX 75231
Publishes low-fat cookbooks, lifestyle guides, and Spanish-language brochures.
http://www.americanheart.org

American Institute for Cancer Research
1759 R Street NW
Washington, DC 20009
The free brochure *The New American Plate* tells how to eat more plant-based foods—and enjoy them!
www.aicr.org

American Society for Nutritional Sciences
9650 Rockville Pike
Bethesda, MD 20814
Publishes *The Journal of Nutrition*.
www.nutrition.org

Cancer Information Service National Cancer Institute
Building 31, Room 10A16
9000 Rockville Pike
Bethesda, MD 20892
Publishes *What You Need to Know about Stomach Cancer*.
http://cis.nci.nih.gov

Center for Nutrition Policy and Promotion
U.S. Department of Agriculture
1120 20th Street NW, Suite 200, North Lobby
Washington, DC 20036

Publishes *Nutrition and Your Health: Dietary Guidelines for Americans*.
www.usda.gov/cnpp

FDA Center for Food Safety and Applied Nutrition
200 C Street SW
Washington, DC 20204
Provides information on food additives, regulations, and more.
http://vm.cfsan.fda.gov/list.html

Food Allergy Network
10400 Eaton Place, Suite 107
Fairfax, VA 22030
Bimonthly newsletter is *Food Allergy News*.
www.foodallergy.org

Food and Nutrition Service
U.S. Department of Agriculture
3101 Park Center Drive, Room 819
Alexandria, VA 22301
Provides fact sheets and an e-mail newsletter.
www.fns.usda.gov/fns

Gluten Intolerance Group of North America
15110 10th Avenue SW, Suite A
Seattle, WA 98166
Publishes a quarterly newsletter and information on celiac disease.
www.gluten.net

International Food Information Council
1100 Connecticut Avenue NW
Suite 430
Washington, DC 20036

Find out the latest in scientific research on food and nutrition.
http://ificinfo.health.org/

National Association of Anorexia Nervosa and Associated Disorders
P.O. Box 7
Highland Park, IL 60035
Publishes quarterly bulletin *Working Together*.
www.anad.org

National Center for Complementary and Alternative Medicine
National Institutes of Health
NCCAM Clearinghouse
P.O. Box 8218
Silver Spring, MD 20907
Publishes fact sheets about herbal supplements and cancer treatments.
http://nccam.nih.gov

National Cholesterol Education Program
Information Center
4733 Bethesda Avenue
Bethesda, MD 20814-4820
Provides nutrition information to health-care professionals and the public.
http://www.nhlbi.nih.gov/about/ncep/index.htm

National Digestive Diseases Information Clearinghouse
2 Information Way
Bethesda, MD 20892-3570
Publications on diabetes, digestive diseases, and metabolic disorders.
www.niddk.nih.gov/health/nddic.htm

National Food Processors Association
1401 New York Avenue NW
Washington DC 20005
The nation's largest food trade association.
www.nfpa.org

National Osteoporosis Foundation
1232 22nd Street NW
Washington, DC 20037
Subscribe to the *Bone Health Updates* newsletter.
www.nog.org

National Pancreas Foundation
P.O. Box 935
Wexford, PA 15090
Ask a question on the Web site and a physician will answer.
www.pancreasfoundation.org

Vegetarian Resource Group
P.O. Box 1463
Baltimore, MD 21203
Everything you ever wanted to know about eating vegetarian.
www.vrg.org

Weight Control Information Network (WIN)
1 WIN Way
Bethesda, MD 20892
Fact sheets and a quarterly newsletter on nutritional disorders.
www.niddk.nih.gov/health/nutrit/nutrit.html

INDEX

Page numbers in *italics* refer
to illustrations.